SEXUAL ASTROLOGY

MARTINE

A DELL BOOK

Published by
Dell Publishing
a division of
Bantam Doubleday Dell Publishing Group, Inc.
1540 Broadway
New York, New York 10036

ISBN: 0-440-18020-1

Reprinted by arrangement with
The Dial Press
Printed in the United States of America
One Previous Dell Edition
September 1979

40 39 38 37 36 35 34 33

OPM

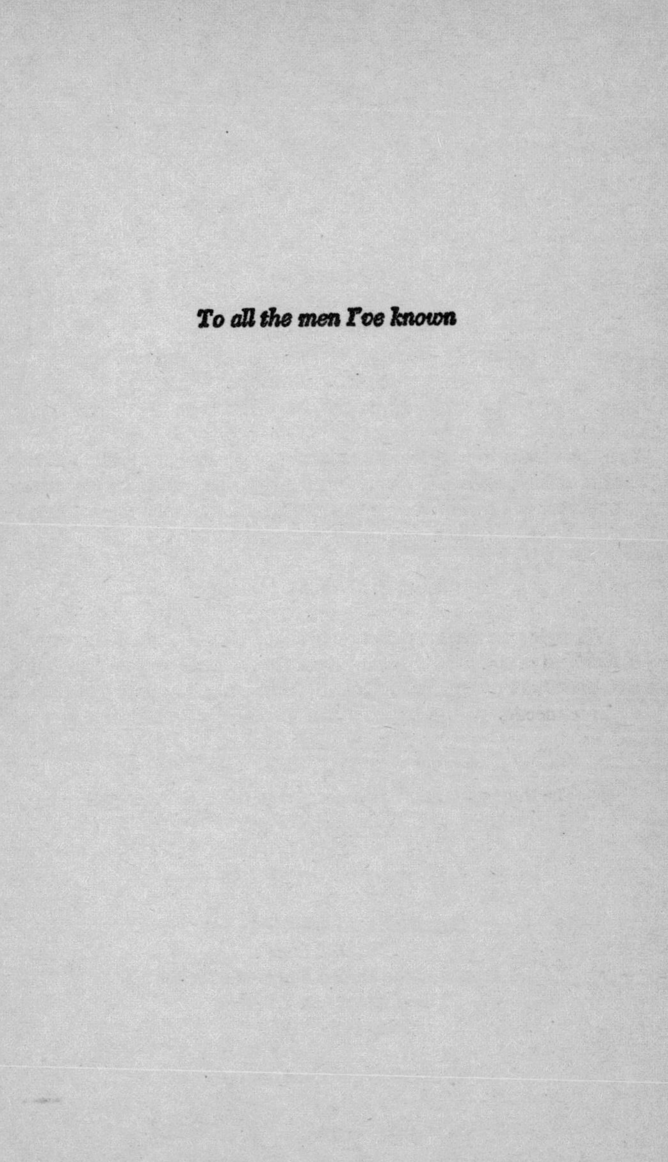

To all the men I've known

CONTENTS

INTRODUCTION

This book deals directly and frankly with a problem of chief concern to every man and woman—sex.

When you were born the sun, the moon, and the stars were in a pattern that will not be witnessed again in your lifetime. That pattern is your horoscope. Astrologers work out in a horoscope the exact position of the stars at the moment of your birth. However, until very recently, it was impossible for them to deal frankly with sexual matters. So they limited themselves to predicting your future, analyzing your character, informing you about your prospects in finance, health, and—romance.

There is nothing wrong with romance, mind you, but anyone who has graduated out of the moonlight and roses relationship to the opposite sex can tell you that it is definitely *not* the same as sex. Romance and sex have distinct and separate identities, and it is simply wrong to confuse one with the other.

My concern is to tell you about sex and astrology. And I mean the *physical* action, the kind of sex that makes the world go around. (If it were a movie, *Sexual Astrology* would probably be X rated.)

Can astrology really provide guidance in sex? Yes. Absolutely yes. This most ancient of sciences will tell you the whole sexual truth and nothing but the truth. You haven't been told until now simply because of moral and legal prohibitions. But "morality" and "the law" vary from one generation to the next. Among the ancient Egyptians, pharaohs had to marry their sisters in order to sustain the truly royal line. An astrologer who condemned incestuous practices in the pharaohs' day would probably have been put to death for violating "the law." All he did was chart the sexual inclinations of the pharaoh and his intended by finding out how Mars and Venus were at work and whether the Sun and Moon were harnessing the proper emotional tides. He would know when Mars (male) was positive and Venus (female) was receptive, and when the masculine Sun and feminine Moon were pulling together to create the ideal physical relationship.

These basic influences cannot be denied. That is why astrology, intelligently applied, can be most useful in helping you to develop your sexual skills, to recognize your most congenial partners, and to practice those sex techniques most likely to give you supreme satisfaction. In this book all is explicitly set down.

While you have a tendency toward some specific sexual action, there are, of course, no two members of any sign who are exactly alike in their responses. No two people even of the same sign will react the same way in the same situation. This is not only a question of free will—which exists—but of such problems as your Moon sign, your Ascendant, and whether you were born within the cusp and therefore must consider the power of a new approaching sign or how much the old sign's declining influence still has.

In writing my regular monthly column for *Viva* magazine, I deal explicitly with sex techniques and practices in relation to astrology. Many, many readers have written me to say that, while I am accurate in general descriptions of their sexual behavior, I go overboard when discussing the kinky variations to which their sign is subject. That is a misunderstanding. Obviously no astrologer can tell any individual whether he will use French ticklers or Japanese boxes, prefer cunnilingus or fellatio, or any other specific sexual action. What *can* be told is whether a particular Sun sign has a tendency to influence those born under it toward certain forms of extreme behavior. Sex is a form of creative energy and therefore directly reacts to the control of cosmic forces. Whether the individual ever realizes that he has certain latent inclinations, however, has more to do with his environment and education, the kind of morality to which he is subject.

I have not felt it necessary to emphasize this point time and again throughout the pages of the book. The reader will have enough intelligence to realize that for himself.

I think the time is ready for this book. It could have been written any time in the past six thousand years by almost any well-trained astrologer. It is long overdue.

Here it is.

ARIES

March 21–April 19

THE FEMALE

Be on guard. The Aries female is sometimes hard to figure out. She seems remote, cool, slightly antipathetic, and you may get the impression she doesn't like men. But that doesn't mean she isn't interested in you.

What's the answer? It's all in the performance. She beguiles you into thinking about her in one way while she knows all the time that she is quite different.

She is a consummate actress, changeable, charming, contradictory, and temperamental, and has the ability to shift emotional gears so quickly that she'll leave a slow-reacting male behind in a swirl of dust. A man has to put up with her desires, which are subject to drastic change. She is impulsive in speech and often doesn't seem to care what she says. Her dynamic restlessness will keep any male on the move.

If you can't keep up, she'll show her impatience. Her temper should have red stickers all over it warning the unwary: *Beware!* Her judgments are swift, sometimes cruel, and she doesn't always think twice before leaping in to deal verbal injury.

Once she is aroused, look out. This woman can scream and claw until she draws blood. She is a raging tigress that cannot be tamed until she is satisfied. If you can't cope, stay away. This is no place for amateurs or the faint of heart.

She has a tendency to be domineering, to impose her opinions on those around her. She'll try to push you around, and her aggressiveness may ward off your advances. But if you are strong enough to butt head-on into her Ram charge and hurl it back—congratulations! You'll find she's well worth the effort.

Aries women are usually playful. They appear to be fearless, even devil-may-care, and they enjoy physical activity. Skiing, tennis, sailing, making love—it's all done with great joy and delight in using their bodies.

She is in love with love, a romanticist, one who accepts sex as one of the pleasures of living. But she wants it direct, and don't try that paternal business. Ms. Aries is looking for a lover, not a father. As a mate she's ardent, loyal, sentimental, and earthy.

Just because she seems to be spontaneous, enterprising, enthusiastic, is no reason to believe that the Aries woman is flibberty-gibbet. She is often an idealist and a thinker, but don't expect her to be "reasonable" or to think things over. When she says go, she means it. For this reason, the women under the sign of Aries attract men. They seem always to be where the action is and are constantly stimulating others to go, go, go.

There is much to admire in her, and she *does* like to be admired. Flattery will get you everywhere with her. She loves to be told what a beautiful body she possesses, and she finds it difficult to pass a mirror without stopping to reassess her personal appearance. She won't go heavy on makeup, but she does think she's beautiful. Your gift to an Aries woman does not have to be practical as long as it's exciting. You can give her provocative lingerie or a filmy nightgown, though she prefers to sleep in the nude. She loves the sensuous feel of her own body.

The Aries woman enjoys the crowds she attracts. For her the scene is always wild, and it will take a bright male to corral a woman like this. He will need energy to keep up with her. The man who marries her, or joins her pack, will have to accept a position as second-in-command or else dig in for a hundred-years' war.

Aries women do have trouble in marriage. Usually the trouble centers around their air of independence and their spending habits. They believe money is made to be spent. Charge accounts are liable to get out of hand and checking accounts out of whack. She thinks that if the money isn't there today, it will be tomorrow—and she's willing to let the future take care of itself. It will take more than a financially agile husband to squirm out of the difficulties she can incur. And this can be a strain on his good nature.

Women born under this sign do not lose their sparkle with age. They may slow down a bit, but they are always way ahead of their sisters born under other signs. They are incurably romantic and, while age reins them a bit, they are always ready to go. They look forward to tomorrow and are quite optimistic that the next day will be a better one.

The male who attaches himself to her may be in for arguments, spending sprees, violent sexual encounters, jealousy, extra-marital affairs, intolerance, egotism, and bad temper.

However, depending on the influence of other planets, the Aries woman can also be the ultimate dream of femininity. You should know the full chart of the Aries woman before you become serious about her—or, more important, before *she* becomes serious about you!

Make no mistake: She's a lot of woman.

HER SEX LIFE

She won't keep you in the dark about her intentions, and in the dark her intentions are wonderful. That's where her secret sexual fantasies flower into erotic delights. She is wholly sensual, feminine, and passionate. When she gives herself, it is more for her pleasure than yours.

She will have sex just about anywhere that suits her purpose. The back of a car will do as well as an office couch or a motel room. When the spell is on her, don't look for subtleties. By the time the soft lights are ready and the sweet music playing, you may already be flat on your back with your pants around your ankles. And she'll have her clothes off, waiting for the action to begin. This woman not only knows what she wants but knows how to get it. Once a poor male is in her sights, he is helplessly swept along.

The way to handle her is to be firm, to meet her aggressiveness head-on. Don't let her push you around. But if you once get in the driver's seat, you had better deliver.

Her appetites are voracious, even animalistic, and she needs a partner who can deal stroke for stroke. If the Ram woman doesn't get enough sexual satisfaction, she will go her own way. The husband or boy friend who is trying to follow a less demanding schedule of his own will see less and less of her. She has too many opportunities for sexual gratification to bother with an apathetic lover.

She likes to be in complete control of the sex act, the one who calls the signals. In the prone position, she is usually the one on top. If she utilizes the sitting position, the man reclines under her; she eases herself down and controls the body movements. If the man sits in a chair, she will sit on his lap; if he lies on the bed with his feet dangling, she will move up to him in her own good time. Her key is control. She wants to virtually dictate the process toward orgasm.

You can expect her to shout, scream, groan, scratch, bite, and claw. If you don't care about scars, give the Aries woman full play. But check the length of her fingernails first. Aries women tend to like things with sharp edges, so she may have long and finely pointed nails. And you don't want the bed to look like a bloody battlefield when you're done!

While there is an element of jealousy in the Aries woman, it comes from injured pride rather than possessiveness. She will probably have many short but intense affairs, for she is basically a primitive, headstrong individual with an animalistic sex drive. She is absolutely miserable when there is no man in her life or when she has just had a quarrel with the man who is her number one. Quarrels can be frequent, for, as I've indicated, Aries women have fiery tempers and are guilty of hasty judgments. They can make a husband or lover quite unhappy.

An Aries female will pick the father of her children very carefully. She will forsake a sexy truck driver or grocery clerk for a dull engineer or attorney. But in coitus, she is not so calculating. Once into the sex act, she goes all out because she enjoys sex so much. She has a healthy interest in her own pleasure; therefore she is receptive to whatever techniques may be employed to add to her enjoyment. This sign rules the passions, and in the throes of sexual emotion there is almost nothing she will not do.

She loves to do what is shocking or forbidden. The boredom that sets in so easily for the active Aries woman is nowhere so apparent as in her sex life. This can lead her into active sexual sadism. For her, this often means the use of leather belts or whips to subjugate the male. The bizarre-looking woman wearing high boots with spike heels, rubber clothes, leather gloves, etc., is usually an Aries woman getting her kicks. She will walk on a lover to inflict pain, whip him, force him (at least, in her make-believe world she'll be forcing him) to commit cunnilingus. The object is to humiliate the male, to receive total satisfaction where he receives none. She will use her body to tease him, and when he reacts to her he will be rewarded with a blow from a cane or the stinging lash of a whip. This master–slave relationship gives her orgasm after orgasm.

She may go to a further extreme by tying up her partner's testicles with a loop of rough cord and yanking it at her leisure. Another loop may be coiled about the penis in conjunction with the testicles, or separately, and the cords pulled to extract the level of pain that gives her the most enjoyment. Or she may strap a dildo to her waist and enter the man from the rear while she works the cords, whips, and other implements at hand. She may wear spurs on her high-heeled boots and sit astride the man while he is on all fours. When she wants him to move forward, she digs in her spurs; when she wants him to stop, she pulls on the reins (a rope tied around his mouth). Because she can wrap her legs halfway around his body, those spurs hit awfully close to his genitals.

To enhance her image as a desirable female, she will go to extremes in sexual dress. Wearing a black lace garter belt and long black stockings with nothing in between, or putting on a bra with cutouts in the cups to reveal her breasts and nipples are some of her more restrained costumes. The idea is always to make the man desperate to possess her.

If she has what she considers a most enjoyable evening or weekend, you, you lucky man, will be invited again. But you'd better keep coming up with something new and diverting. Or you will lose one of the most interesting sex partners in the zodiac.

THE MALE

If your boy friend, lover, or husband was born under the sign of the Ram, you may already be aware that your man is aggressive, energetic, and restless. He doesn't move. He swashbuckles. He may be impractical and impulsive, but he's imaginative and dynamic. He makes things happen. If you go out with an Aries, you never know exactly where you'll wind up. But wherever you do, it will be exciting. You also know that he may be generous one moment and stingy the next. He can drive you crazy, but you love it.

You love it because the man born under the sign of Aries exudes sex. He has a dominating personality impatient with rules and conventions. Here is a man who is not interested in the man-above-woman position when he climbs into bed. (*If* he climbs into bed. The man born under the sign of the Ram may want to have intercourse on the top of a car, in a moving power boat, or in a crowded bus!)

You'll get all the excitement and pleasure you want and perhaps a little more than you can take. There'll be fun a-plenty, but it's a little like playing croquet with live bombs. Any minute something may explode in your face.

He is jealous. He wants all of you, even if you can't have all of him. The Aries man may be a bed bouncer, but he expects loyalty and fidelity from his woman. If she wanders from the straight and narrow, that will wreck the romance. He is jealous of everyone from his closest friend to the TV repairman.

Don't tell an Aries man that you want time to think things over—he wants to hear only one word from a girl: yes! And don't worry about what happens then. His pride is not going to let you off with just a wham, bam, thank you ma'am. Once he's whisked you into the bedroom, he may not allow you to take your clothes off. He may rip them off. He's anxious to get going. But he won't leave you disappointed, and he certainly won't bore you. You'll probably have a night that you won't forget very soon.

You can keep him around afterward by saying nice things about his technique—he's a sucker for flattery if it's not too obvious. But remember: The Aries man is not stupid. He's simply so impressed with himself he's likely to believe flattery is no more than understatement.

If you prefer a more domestic, quiet life, Aries is not a satisfactory mate. He's a trailblazer. Yet beneath all the dash and glamor you may glimpse a curious vulnerability—the appeal of a small boy who needs a mother to watch over him. Anyone who sees through his surface glitter knows how to win his heart. He will be loyal, sincere, and affectionate to the person he loves.

He has a fine sense of humor and likes women to be intelligent as well as attractive. He is clever and quick at repartee, which he uses to deflate pretense or affectation in others.

He is a capable executive, forthright but insistent on having his own way. He will probably make a great deal of money but won't be as successful at holding on to it. He enjoys extravagance too much and believes that spending money is a way of demonstrating power.

Your problem will be keeping up with him. But you'll want to.

HIS SEX LIFE

The key to his sexual behavior is impulsiveness. What he needs to learn is the give and take of a true sexual union. He is intolerant of opposition to any of his sexual fantasies.

Don't attempt to be a tease. If you promise, you'd better deliver. If you don't intend to bed the man, sit home and watch the late show. Aries doesn't play games. And if you're not prepared to perform the kind of innovative acts that until now you've only read about in books, stay home and practice your knitting. Anything that smacks of the routine will bore him just this side of hysteria. If you want to please an Aries man sexually, you will have to use your imagination—and no holds are barred.

He won't worry about consequences. When he wants you, he wants you. If you have an affair with this man, always plan ahead and have your diaphragm or IUD in place. Or be sure you've taken your birth-control pills. He may have a condom somewhere, but don't expect him to use it.

Do expect him to carry the action. You may have suggestions, but if he accepts your ideas, he'll carry them a bit further. For instance, if you suggest that he suck on your nipple, don't be surprised if in a short time he's licking your navel, tonguing your clitoris, or working on the area between the vagina and the anus. Be prepared to expect the unexpected. His untamed drive delights in attempting the shocking and forbidden. Aries men are explorers who must run the show. Thwarted, they become irritable. Positions will vary depending on his age, but at any age he is young in spirit. He always prefers the dominating position.

And he won't stop short at sadism.

For example, he won't be satisfied to get his kicks just from your oral stimulation. You can expect him to start tugging your hair, pinching your nipples, or ramming his penis into your mouth to the point of discomfort. If you can derive satisfaction from this, accept it without a whimper, for it will increase his pleasure.

A favorite position is to place you on your knees leaning forward. At this point, he can enter the vagina or the anus. You may be surprised! However, no matter what his decision, he will expect you to cooperate. This basic position may take on variations, such as kneeling and leaning over a stool, couch, or bed, or standing and bending over, using the furniture as a support while he approaches you from the rear.

An alternate position of the man-above-woman may find you with your shoulders touching the bed, or floor, as he raises your buttocks with his hands and approaches on his knees to spear you either in the vagina or the anus.

When an Aries male reaches middle-age he finds that he is not as potent as in his younger years. A wrong word at the wrong time will lead to temporary impotence—a particularly horrible blow for him. He will react in his usual aggressive fashion, probably by starting a dozen flirtations and romances with women half his age. He'll be trying to prove that he is the man he always was. And if he can't prove he's the man he used to be, it can lead to a breakdown.

In his prime, however, beware of his aggressiveness and of his tendency (remember, I am always describing *tendencies*) to actually enjoy giving pain. He will enter a woman before she is ready, just to enjoy feeling her flinch. In oral technique he is rough and ready. During cunnilingus, don't be surprised if he bites and sucks hard on the clitoris.

Or he may swing to the far side of the spectrum and complete his coitus with whips and canes. He especially enjoys spanking a woman before intercourse, and not only with the palm of his hand. He'll use a hair brush, a Ping-Pong paddle, a bamboo cane. If he finds a willing female, he will paddle her bottom until the skin is raspberry red and tears stream from her eyes. Her pleading or begging for mercy only excites him to further cruelties—and better orgasms. The more noise, the better he likes it. In some cases he may use a whip and leave welts on his partner's body. His aim is submission.

If he has enough money to spend on "equipment," he may have a special room complete with chains attached to the wall. These chains have shackles that bind a woman's hands and legs so that he can bite or pinch her nipples and have intercourse with her at his will. A few whiplashes usually melt away any resistance to whatever adventure he may be ready for.

One Aries man I know has a favorite game he calls

Horsey. The woman is on all fours, and he uses a rope on her as a rein and bit. He enters through her anal opening. She moves forward slowly on her hands and knees, and every now and then he pulls back on the rope, *hard.*

Naturally, other signs in the zodiac have differing effects on the Aries individual, and men born under this sign will vary from one extreme to the other. But they are extremists. So, girls, beware! If you run across a "pure" Aries, be prepared to run to the nearest exit if his sexual needs show signs of becoming just a little too much.

Or stay—and enjoy. That depends on you, and *your* sign.

One way to handle him is to sixty-nine it. Then you're always in a position to say, "Look, we don't want to hurt each other—*do we?*"

Group sex doesn't faze our man. The more, the merrier. In fact, you can bet that the wife-swapping in the neighborhood was started by an Aries man. He likes to show off his sexual prowess, and he will usually come up with ideas that are a little far out and even seem on the kooky side to the others present. One exception. He will not play the passive partner in the anal sex game. Not that this offends his sexual sensibilities, but that position is a threat to his "manhood." After all, that is what "fags" do.

There is a tendency to sadism among many a man born under the sign of the Ram.

FIRST MOVES

You have to be sincere, for they have a discerning eye for the phony. It's safe to open the conversation on an intellectual note. They think of themselves as people of reason rather than emotion, and believe you respect them if you appeal to them through their intelligence. On the other hand, they respect *you* if you make no attempt to boss them or force your opinions on them. Go to them with your problems and you will find them cooperative and understanding.

You'll find them where the action is, in a place that's different: the bar that has a special atmosphere, the cocktail party that is out of the ordinary, the unusual excursion to any place that promises adventure. Aries is looking for excitement. They are original and will seize upon a new idea. In fact, presenting them with a new idea is an "open sesame" to their affections. If such an idea gets their attention, they'll be off to blaze a trail. They are involved with theater, music, and the local museum—usually among the leaders and surrounded by admirers.

One clue to spotting an Aries: look for those who simply can't pass a mirror without stopping to admire their reflection. Others do this occasionally—Aries always does.

A good preliminary gambit: make a suggestion of an intellectual nature. Offer to lend them an exciting new book or to go with them to a new art exhibition or a play that's just opened. Show them you share their interests.

After you've made a date with an Aries, never be late. That will really start you off on the wrong cloven hoof. They place a great deal of importance on punctuality.

A woman dating an Aries man can expect to be taken to sporting events. While he places more emphasis on sports *participation*, he can and does appreciate spectator sports also. As a participant, look for him in the more active sports: boxing, fencing, skiing, tobogganing, the discus, and the javelin. Try to say something subtly flattering about his athletic skills.

If you want to get along with Aries, there is no doubt you're better off as a follower than a leader.

Just say yes sir or yes ma'am to these "first sergeants" of the zodiac.

Don't plan an evening ahead with an Aries: let him or her lead you.

The following tips may help:

If you play records, choose music with a definite fast beat. Save waltzes and fiddles for someone else.

If you're meeting at your place, have some food handy, because a night that starts at 1:00 A.M. may be going strong at 5:00. Ariens are noted for their powers of endurance. Hunger pangs will hit long before the sandman calls an end to the evening.

Because the Arien is impetuous and impatient, keep whatever precautions you think will be necessary within easy reach. Also keep towels, creams, and lotions that you may want to use handy. If your date is a long-fingernailed Aries woman, you may want to keep some antiseptics handy. She will especially enjoy your wincing as she applies the lotion afterward. An Aries male may or may not wait until you're ready for him, so have your jellies ready when he's ready for his jollies. Don't think he's going to read a book while you go searching the bathroom for a tube of whatdyacallit that you are sure you had someplace in the cabinet—or was it in the dresser?

Pace yourself. Both the male and female Arien are naturally aggressive, and if you try to keep up with all the activity, you'll be left panting and exhausted too early in the evening. Try to relax, and you'll enjoy yourself more.

EROGENOUS ZONES

The nerve endings especially sensitive in the Aries man and woman are in the head and face. Ariens will respond to gentle stroking of the forehead or playing with the hair of the scalp. This can take the form of combing or just gently caressing the top of the head. Run a finger lightly over the temple of the Arien, or through his hair, and you have the beginning of sexual friendship. Ear nibblers will find a willing response from Aries, and the woman especially will go wild if you blow in her ear. A lip nibbler gets results, and a light kiss on the closed eye for some reason will send shudders and spasms of joy up her Arien spine.

Bussing by a bearded man gives Aries woman a thrill. The soft hair of the man's beard is like a thousand sensations delighting her nerve endings. If you don't have a beard, don't worry about it. Simply touching her lips with your fingertips will create wild sensations.

For the Aries man, run your fingers lightly over his lips from end to end, using a circular motion. The results may startle you—but don't say you weren't warned!

LAST MOVES

When the clock starts ticking overtime on the affair, the way out is the same as the way in. How did you meet your Aries? Steer him or her back to the meeting, to the gathering, to the party, get them back among admirers, encourage the introductions, sit back and watch them operate. The moths will quickly flutter around Aries's magnetic personality. Chances are that after the first party, you will be on your own, for with any sort of encouragement Aries tends to move on.

If the party doesn't work, go to bed with a good book whenever Aries is in the mood for something exciting. If you simply must go out, leave the midnight bash at ten because you're feeling "exhausted."

Give "practical" gifts. Stick to a routine. Become

impatient with their demands and self-indulgences. Disagree.

You'll be home free.

Alone.

YOUR SENSUAL GUIDE

ARIES and ARIES: Usually what will happen in sexual encounters is that the woman will dominate the male. An Aries man won't long be content with a subordinate role. There will be competition as each tries to take the lead, and this causes an increasing number of temperamental fireworks. Eventually this means unresponsive disharmony in the bedroom. Initially, a promising affair. A poor prognosis for marriage.

ARIES and TAURUS: Aries wants to make love on impulse. The cautious deliberateness of Taurus, who rarely does anything on impulse, will prove annoying. If Taurus can allow Aries to lead the way, they can discover new possibilities of sensual enjoyment. Otherwise, it's hard to establish a desirable balance. An affair will develop considerable friction. And they're really not suited for the long haul.

ARIES and GEMINI: This union can be exciting, for both are restless, active, willing to explore. The tendency of Aries to dominate is curbed by Gemini's adroitness. Gemini suffers no sexual inhibitions, but its high-spirited energy may seek other outlets for fulfillment. An affair will last as long as Gemini maneuvers successfully. Marriage may settle Gemini down and prove quite successful.

ARIES and CANCER: A powerful sexual attraction is usual between these two signs. The trouble is that when the passions are spent, there is little left. Aries doesn't find enough compensations, and they begin to argue over trifles. Temperamental unsuitability leads to further incompatibility in bed. The forecast for an affair is heavy seas, and for a marriage, it's almost certain shipwreck.

ARIES and LEO: Aggressive Aries finds its equal in Leo, whose frank and outgoing sexuality is fully a match. Sex is usually straightforward, without kinky proclivities. That doesn't mean it can't be fiery. Aries must be sure to flatter Leo on its physical performance. Leo must be sure not to deflate Aries too much in restraining this sign's inherent tendency to dominate. Otherwise, all signals are go.

ARIES and VIRGO: The boldness of Aries is likely to capture the fancy of reserved Virgo. But their sexual personalities are so dissimilar that a good deal of tolerance is required on both sides. Aries will be charmed by the tact, reticence, and control of Virgo. Virgo may not approve of Aries's extravagant ideas about lovemaking. An affair will be intermittent fun, but the chance for success in marriage is no better than fifty-fifty.

ARIES and LIBRA: They can develop a short-term affinity. Aries's aggressiveness may uncover a streak of unconventionality in Libra. Both love sexual pleasure, but Aries will probably try to go too far too fast. Libra tends to be idealistic and can be disillusioned. They should practice refinement in the nuances of carnal behavior. A fulfilling physical union will make a success of an affair but not a marriage.

ARIES and SCORPIO: Sex can be stimulating or frustrating. Those are the two ways it can go. Both are biased toward action, blessed with great physical energy.

But they are both independent and aspire to control. Prolonged disputes will test even the phenomenal ability of a shared passion to keep them happy. Scorpio's jealousy is also a danger. An affair will be unstable, a marriage will be unconventional.

ARIES and SAGITTARIUS: Both are a little combative, so there will be plenty of conflict in the sexual arena. Aries's optimism and good humor may overcome Sagittarius's tendency toward moodiness and bring out a playful attitude toward making love. The camaraderie of the bedroom can cast a benevolent aura over the rest of the relationship. A rewarding affair. Marriage will be linked closely to the satisfaction of physical desires.

ARIES and CAPRICORN: Aries is forward-looking, anxious to experiment. Capricorn is more of a prude. Capricorn may prefer one way of having intercourse or even a settled time for it, and its passions are more restrained. However, Aries can upset Capricorn's calculations, awakening the strong libido of its sex partner. If so, auguries are good—better for marriage than for a short-term affair.

ARIES and AQUARIUS: The physical relationship will be both energetic and innovative. It is probable that Aries will dominate, since Aquarius is more passive by nature. Aquarius will not give in, though, nor accept a domination that does not seem to be in its best interests. Aries needs tact to deal with this highly emotional dreamer. An unusual, eventful affair and—granted mutual understanding—a most rewarding marriage.

ARIES and PISCES: Aries will be intrigued by Pisces's almost physically intuitive boudoir behavior. Aries's vivacious confidence will draw Pisces out of its shy shell. Pisces's sexual fantasies, put into practice, can be very stimulating. They should have some buoyantly joyful sessions together. Prospects for either an affair or a marriage are good if they work out temperamental differences.

TAURUS

April 20–May 20

THE FEMALE

Venus is her ruler, so she knows all the arts of seduction without the aid of textbooks. When she innocently crosses her legs she sends out SEX signals to every male in the room. If she really wants to interest a man, she merely moves her erotic antennae in his direction. Unless the man is dead, he will react!

As a sensualist, she is nonpareil in drawing men to her. But while many are called, few are chosen. She can be rather conventional about yielding too quickly. Again, she relies on her intuitions about a potential lover, and these can be complex and deep. The heart has its reasons.

She is quite sentimental, and quickly becomes possessive. With her, the course of true love will not run smoothly. She is innately jealous, quite capable of staging a stormy scene that would put Hollywood's best special-effects men to shame. If she feels neglected, she won't make her point by indirect or artful means—not this gal! She'll say exactly what is on her mind. She may end up breaking crockery over your head, just by way of emphasis.

The Taurus woman knows what she wants, and in her obstinacy can become unreasonable. When she is after something, she is determined to get it, even if it means that she must resort to tears, threats, or throwing things. If you are linked with a Taurean woman, be prepared to give in—or get out.

Scorned, she is a bad enemy. She will use any weapon at her command to get revenge. On the other hand, she is willing to give as well as to take. She is very affectionate but possesses a native shrewdness. Quick to spot a fraud, she responds instinctively to sincerity in others.

She relies on her emotions. Some people make the

mistake of underrating her intelligence because it is not the kind that displays itself in social repartee. She has a rarer form of intelligence: She knows that to uncover the truth you have to trust your intuitions.

She is practical, not idealistic. You won't find her mooning over a hero on a movie screen when a much more accessible man is sitting right beside her. She doesn't believe in platonic love; for her, love only exists in tandem with physical attraction.

When she is young, the Taurus woman is hungry to learn about "life," and the man who can teach her has the best chance to win her. However, the more she learns about men, the more particular she becomes about choosing lovers. She sets up guidelines, and if the man doesn't measure up, she won't let him get far.

She's a sensuous female and if a mate cannot satisfy her, she feels no guilt about looking elsewhere. She doesn't try to rationalize her sexual need. It is enough for her that the need exists.

The Taurus woman dresses well, in good taste, but not lavishly. She knows how to buy within a budget and get the most out of what she spends. She *loves* jewelry. The Taurus woman often wears rings, earrings, and she especially favors necklaces. Her neck and throat are very sensitive, and adorning this area brings her exceptional pleasure.

She appreciates luxury. A man who can keep her awash in fur and emeralds, surround her with the visible signs of wealth, will keep her heart forever.

Unfortunately, she is apt to become careless. When she feels at home with you, sure of herself, she becomes lazy, sloppy in her dress, late in her appointments. Since, like her male counterpart, she also enjoys food and drink, she may get plump. Or fat. Inside every lean Taurus female there is a fat one trying to get out.

She needs an outlet for her affections, but because

of inbred conservatism she will look for it in marriage rather than an affair. She wants someone dependable who will stand by her. Weak-willed men don't attract her. However, she is likely to treat a loved one as a possession and not make the effort needed to insure his loyalty.

Even though her emotional reactions are strong, her control is stronger. She will almost never show affection in public. And although you can turn her on, she can deny her own desires and hold out as long as her common sense dictates.

Taurus female may look fragile and helpless, but she's not. She is always stubborn and persistent.

She is a good cook, a good bedmate, and can make a good wife, for she is extremely loyal and loving. However, a word of caution: She will *never* forgive infidelity. If you have a roving eye, don't take up with her. You'll regret it.

She is the quintessential woman. Treat her like one.

HER SEX LIFE

A woman born under Taurus has invited you to a candlelit dinner. She has the proper wines. She has made an excellent dinner. Conversing, you note she has a lovely voice (many Taurean woman sing very well). You are entranced by her gown and the well-matched jewelry.

She has found something attractive in you too, or you wouldn't be there. And you're going to get the full treatment.

You note that her skin is soft and glowing, a general asset of all Taurus women, and her low neckline reveals full breasts, for most Taurus women are curvaceous. Later you dance, and her perfume snares you further. She has chosen the ambiance for this romantic rendezvous with care. The whole evening is the product of a well-studied plan. In the bedroom the lights are soft and the sheets are silk, for Taurus women have an affinity for silk rather than linen or cotton.

You must lead her gently. She expects you to be kind and patient and to make love by the book. She expects to be pleased by sex and is not interested in unusual approaches. If you want to develop new techniques, you will have to do so gradually, after she has confidence in you. While she has a tremendous capacity for sexual experiences, she is set in her ways and difficult to change.

The Taurus woman is a demanding lover. One way or another, you will deliver when you get her (or she finally takes you) to bed. She'll leave you breathless. After all, this is the arena where she functions best. Every encounter has the intensity of a *corrida*.

She welcomes minor signals of affection—a hug, a squeeze of the buttocks, a kiss—but you won't keep her placated with those for long. What's the use of tuning up the strings if you aren't going to play?

Her boudoir behavior is incurably and profoundly romantic. The setting must always be right. She loves fur, and may like to make love on a fur bedspread or on a fur coat spread on the floor. She'll always look her seductive best. When she makes her entrance into the bedroom wearing nothing but perfume and jewels, you'll know it's mating time. This tyger burns brightest in the bedroom!

Her favorite technique is to dramatize her vivid sexual fantasies. To heighten eroticism, she'll pretend to resist—provided you cooperate as a ruthless, not-to-be-denied lover. Or she'll descend on you like a vampire on a sleeping victim. It's all make-believe, a strong healthy expression of real passion.

But she can go to extremes. Taurus woman is torn between a tremendous sexual drive and a need for security. Since the sexual need is great, it can turn her to nymphomania and/or prostitution. She *must* have her gratification.

The older she gets, the more she will let down in her physical appearance. In the beginning, there was a silk sheet on the bed. Now, what turns her on is a dirty blanket stretched over sand or a filthy floor. And she loves those work odors emanating from a man's body.

In Italy, not too long ago, men sometimes carefully wiped the perspiration from around their crotch with a cloth, then placed that cloth in a breast pocket. While dancing or holding the woman close enough, she got the full effect of the odor and was his for the night. A Taurus woman would understand that.

Other hang-ups: Her need for oral gratification inevitably results in an enthusiasm for fellatio.

Some Taurus women turn to lesbianism. Once she tries this form of gratification, however, she finds it difficult to break off. She will go from woman to woman, always looking for a sexier, more satisfactory partner.

The Taurus woman is also subject to hang-ups such as coprophilia, an attraction to filth or dung. She handles the excrement or rubs it on her body. A fortunately small minority of Taurus women suffer from a strong urge to urinate on the male (scatophagy) as part of the sexual foreplay, and some even consider the drinking of urine as an aphrodisiac.

THE MALE

I won't deceive you—he's no one's idea of a tempestuous lover. Patient but forceful would be a better description. He will take his time deciding what he wants. But he will never give up until he gets it.

His passions are slow to focus, but when he finally has you clearly in view—look out! You may have to scramble if you want to get out of his way. You'll probably prefer to stay there and enjoy it.

Don't waste coquetry on him. He'll know you're just being coy. The more you try to con him, the more obstinate he becomes.

If you've known your man for any time, you know he is stubborn. This is, in fact, the most stubborn sign of the zodiac. Don't lock horns with him, because he is not going to yield. He may try to use persuasion if he has an intellectual turn of mind, but if necessary he will finally command. If he is the physical type and you are being difficult, he will communicate his needs even more forcefully. The Taurus male *is* physical. This is part of his attraction. He is earthy, lusty, sensual.

Taurus likes to enjoy his passions in comfort. He will set the lights low, turn on soft music, bring out champagne or brandy. To him the setting is almost as important as the act. He surrounds himself with beautiful things, like fine furniture and paintings, because he wants the best of everything. But if you are in a mood to dilly or dally, he may have a drink or two and be off to sleep while you are still trying to decide. Playing hard to get with Taurus is a waste of time.

He loves good food and drink. In fact, weight is often a problem for Taurean men. A true connoisseur, he doesn't just eat because he's hungry or drink because he's thirsty. He *savors*. This is also true of his sexual appetites, and he appreciates a female who can satisfy his major cravings.

Whether food, drink, or sex, Taurus thinks the best is none too good—or too plentiful. He's not the kind who is content to kiss the air that lately kissed thee. His tastes are ribald and lusty. He is a real man in a real world.

Part of that unswerving doggedness can be traced to his immense confidence in his sexuality. He doesn't have to prove himself as so many men do. As Mark Twain remarked, he has the calm cool courage of a Christian who is holding four aces.

On a date, you'll have a marvelous time. You won't need to pretend to be something other than you are. He'll convince you that what you are is pretty wonderful.

Taurus definitely understands the value of a dollar and wants his money's worth. You can't sell him—he has to buy—and he'll have to be really convinced before he opens his wallet. No one can part Taurus from money—except himself. He'll go along spending sensibly, getting solid value for what he pays, saving for a sunnier day. Then—surprise!—when your birthday comes, you'll get those expensive diamond earrings you've always wanted. Or a pair of tickets, first class, on a round-the-world cruise.

Men who have their Sun in Taurus usually have good common sense. They are constructive and stable and not afraid of hard work. Obstacles only make them more persistent.

Despite his seeming vitality, once a Taurean male develops an illness, recuperation is slow and long. On the other hand, he tends to take better care of himself than men of other signs. He feels instinctively that he must stay well.

Don't try to tell him where to go or what to do. And you won't have to tell him what you want. He doesn't need to know what you want in order to *do* what you want.

Whatever you do, don't provoke a Taurean man. He is slow to anger but once he is aroused, he is furious. Forgiving and forgetting are difficult for him.

Men born under the early part of the Taurus sign love action. They need it and desire it. When they are confronted with a problem, they look for an overt physical solution. (A woman who tries to hold a

Taurus male by threats or blackmail can find herself in serious trouble!)

Taureans born in the latter part of the sign are more likely to employ cunning. Unfortunately, sometimes they are not as cunning as they think they are, and failure can often lead to a deep mental depression.

Taurus male can be jealous. He likes to hold on to all his possessions. He is a tenacious collector and hates to part with anything, even if he no longer regards it as special. If your affair is over, he will try to maintain a strong friendship. But take care! He can be a difficult friend because of a tendency to be overcritical. He is only tolerant of people who do not touch his emotions.

He is stubborn enough to fight for a losing cause but will seldom do anything just for others. He is too self-centered.

Taurus males born under the first two weeks of the sign are usually impatient. They look for immediate results. They will drive hard to their goal, but often with much waste of energy, movement, and excitement, and the needless smashing of small objects on their way.

The Taurus male born in the last two weeks of the sign tends to be helter skelter, to feint and make false passes to confuse the opposition. Their road is less direct and more zigzag—and doesn't always arrive at the intended destination.

Learn from a matador how to handle this bull of a fellow. The matador allows the bull his own side of the arena and does not invade it. He makes the bull come to him.

Taurus is strong willed, strongly sexual, possessive, and intensely emotional. He has a primitive approach to sex that can be especially stimulating. If you have the understanding and the patience, and particularly if you enjoy male protectiveness, this is your man!

HIS SEX LIFE

He enjoys making love. That may sound simple-minded—who doesn't?—but there *are* people who use sex to relieve tension, to establish mastery, to prove virility, or simply as a game they play to keep score. They don't really enjoy it for its own sake.

Taurus does.

In may ways the Taurus man qualifies as an ideal lover. He is sensitive and understands his partner's feelings. He's a self-starter who doesn't need a lot of coaxing and encouragement.

The Taurus male gets his sex urges early. From his adolescence, he thinks and dreams about women. As a young male he is lusty, and his one ambition is to "get his rocks off." Any female is acceptable, for he has a practical approach to sex. His needs are insatiable. But don't worry. He will find ways to help you satisfy him.

His foreplay is studied, almost a theatrical production. There is no spur-of-the-moment intercourse. Not until he feels the moment is at hand will anything happen. He prefers it slow and easy—no wham, bam, thank you ma'am. But he is not particularly imaginative in his lovemaking. Don't look for him to be an exotic guide into unknown avenues of sexual experience. The tried is the true way for him, but he works at it, and you won't be disappointed with the results.

Some people think Taurus male is a bit on the simple side when it comes to intercourse. He likes his sex straight, uncomplicated, and often. A friend of mine, who has a Taurus boy friend, complains of his "innocent sexual exuberance." It isn't a frequently heard complaint, however. That kind of lover is increasingly hard to find.

Stamina? Taurus could wear down a glacier. His

greatest asset is his staying power. What he lacks in imagination, he more than makes up for in his ability to continue. You will have to take the initiative if you want to lead him to try something different in exotic positions. Best bet: cunnilingus. He enjoys oral activity.

A cautioning word: You can't drive a Taurean, you can only suggest. Insistence will just make him turn against you. Taurus is an earth sign and stubborn, and subtle suggestions will work much more readily.

Since the Taurus male loves creature comforts, a bed of fur with soft lights and the stereo filling the room is his idea of sexual heaven. Another suggestion which *especially* pleases: Encourage him to pour a few drops of liquor on your bare skin and lick them off with his tongue. This practice is known to the Turks as *yalamac*. They use their own smoky liquors, but a good scotch will serve. A half-pint should nicely cover the areas in which he is interested.

The man responds to body odors. The smell of a woman's armpit or the scent between her legs will have an aphrodisiacal effect on him. He may even lick the perspiration from the woman's body, although he would doubtless appreciate *yalamac* better. He likes to rub his girl friend down with massage oils before he begins. With his oral fixation, he may start by sucking each of her toes in turn. Don't bother trying to rush him. His ritual is his own, and he will move on his own time. And he is quite likely to work up to cunnilingus as part of his foreplay.

Bisexuality can be a hang-up. Taurus male is capable of handling more than one partner at a time, and sometimes will play mix and match with the sexes. Taureans with a typically strong sex drive may turn to a young man in the afternoon and a woman at night. In either case, he may exhibit a preference for entry at the rear (anilingus), which is also sometimes combined with his proclivity for oral gratification.

Sexual interest in the buttocks (natelism) is common among Taureans.

Recently a Taurus man came to me for consultation about a "sex problem" that is not typical of the Taurus sign. He began by telling me that the evening before he had been with his girl friend and his best friend. He had performed cunnilingus on the woman, fellatio on the man, then copulated with the woman while the man entered him from the rear.

His problem: premature ejaculation!

Cleanliness is not a prerequisite to his sexual enjoyment. He actually gets a sexual charge from entering a house of prostitution that offers dirty sheets, roaches, stifling smells, and a woman who is somewhat less than clean.

Coprophilia, the attraction to filth or dung that is a hang-up of some Taurus women, is something to which Taurus men are also more susceptible than men born under other signs. Extreme cases may insist that the partner join with them in this practice. For some reason, best known to psychiatrists, this kind of activity turns them on. I heard of one man with this particular hang-up who went a step further—he would indulge in this practice only when the feces were served on expensive china!

FIRST MOVES

You won't find Taurus being the life of the party. Look around the fringes for someone who, though silent, appears completely self-possessed. You can often recognize Taurus by the voice, which is low pitched, strongly timbred, soothing to the ear. Or watch everyone's reactions to a disturbing event: a terribly gauche remark, a sudden clumsy gesture—dropping cigarette ash or spilling a drink. The person who hardly blinks an eye, that's Taurus.

Head straight for Taurus if you are looking for an oasis in a desert of insecure, garrulous people. You won't find any social twitchiness here.

It may take a while to arrange a first date. Taurus male won't be quick to ask; Taurus woman won't be quick to accept. When they do, you'll know it's because you're really liked.

A first date? Go to a comedy, something where the humor is on the broad and obvious side. Mel Brooks rather than Jacques Tati, Billy Wilder over Terence Rattigan. Taurus's taste in humor tends to be robust and Falstaffian.

Dining out? The aroma of good cooking, the bouquet of fine wine will get you everywhere with Taurus. Take a Taurus woman to a fine restaurant, let her savor the sauces, the gravies, the ambiance. Try the grand, splashy emporium where the portions are generous. Taurus has a terrific appetite.

The Taurus man enjoys a home-cooked dinner that shows you made a special effort to please him. The old adage that the way to a man's heart is through his stomach could have been written with a Taurus male in mind.

But while Taurus loves good food and fine wine, he or she hates to see money wasted. The fine restaurant should not be needlessly extravagant and should return full value for what you spend. She will respect you for being shrewd with a dollar. In turn, he will appreciate your home cooking more if you haven't splurged on a Beef Wellington but have whipped up a delicious pot roast from less expensive cuts of meat.

Those born under this sign are very materialistic. If your hobby includes collecting things, let them see your collection. If it has a definite commercial value, let him know it. You will be all the more admired.

However, don't lie about it or exaggerate your claims. Taurus hates a liar and can see through a phony.

If you are thinking of giving a gift, try something of a practical nature but with an added touch. An evening coat in a sumptuous fabric that also doubles as rainwear would suit Taurus woman perfectly. Taurus male has very masculine tastes and is also conservative. Since the throat and neck is the sensitive area, he would be pleased with a cashmere or heavy silk scarf. If you want to be extravagant, keep in mind that the emerald is Taurus's gem and is said to bring them luck in love.

Remember: They cannot feed on self-love alone and require proofs of love from others. If you sincerely care about them, show it, let them know it.

EROGENOUS ZONES

The sensitive area for Taurus is the throat and neck. Begin with light finger strokes or caresses at the base of the head, skipping lightly to the neck. Move on to kisses on the throat, and you'll soon cause Taurus to kindle.

The opportunities for "accidental" touches of this kind are endless. While fixing a man's necktie, for example, you can fondle the throat or let your fingernails gently slide over the area. You'll be surprised at his quick reaction!

On the beach, a gentle hand on a woman's bare neck or the dusting of sand from it will send a message to her brain.

In the privacy of your room, the neck and throat area should be the target. Passionate kisses and gentle love bites on the back of the neck will especially arouse Taurus. But, again, don't forget Taurus likes it slow and easy, so keep your approach studied and don't try to force the moment.

LAST MOVES

The longer you are involved with a Taurus, the more difficult getting out of the relationship becomes.

In the beginning, simply not being able to keep up with Taurus's sexual demands may cool the affair. The Taurus woman, unsatisfied, even though she may be understanding, will not put up with you for long.

If you indicate to the Taurus male that there are times you would rather sit quietly and listen to Mozart, he will soon find other companions.

But as the affair progresses, Taurus also tends to look on you as a good friend—and it's hard to break off with a good friend.

At this point, if love has stayed too long and you begin looking for the nearest way to the egress, you will have to run counter to their character. You might become a spendthrift, serve cold, tasteless sandwiches, go dressed in torn and tattered clothes, make rude or tactless remarks.

Don't be guided by what Taurus wants to do but insist on having your own sweet way. In an argument, try your damndest to change Taurus's ways of thinking. Be coarse in speech, extravagant in spending habits. Flirt. Take Taurus away from home frequently with any excuse for socializing. By all means, invite your relatives along.

It may take a little time, but the slow way is sure. Taurus will eventually be frolicking in someone else's pasture.

YOUR SENSUAL GUIDE

TAURUS and ARIES: Two differing personalities. Taurus does not like to be hurried and will be turned off by the enthusiasm of Aries, who tends to enjoy sex in a much more impulsive fashion. Taurus is not sensually imaginative but, if Aries can engage its emotions, will try hard to respond. An affectionate affair can develop, but in marriage Taurus must learn to overlook Aries's occasional infidelities.

TAURUS and TAURUS: They are not always sexually compatible. The woman tends to be sentimental about love, the male more inclined to be earthy. Taurus man actually prefers the company of other males. He also has a roving eye for women. Taurus woman, in turn, hates to be deceived or neglected. An affair can and should be pleasurable, but for marriage the auguries are mixed.

TAURUS and GEMINI: Dualistic, variable, changeable, versatile Gemini is at opposites from steady, persevering Taurus. Taurus is attracted to the artistic and imaginative side of Gemini. And the reticence of Taurus is likely to intrigue Gemini. However, Gemini will be irritated at the slow Taurus reactions and its plodding amatory techniques. A poor affair and not much better as conjugal partners.

TAURUS and CANCER: Taurus finds Cancer a romantic, satisfying partner. Taurus's stability is not shaken by Cancer's moods, and its steadiness of purpose provides firm ground for Cancer's leaning toward procrastination about sex. Both share a strong desire for a passionate emotional life. If the physical side is gratifying, this will be a satisfactory affair and probably a rewarding marriage.

TAURUS and LEO: Taurus will have to go along with Leo's grandeur complex. Leo takes as a matter of right its place at the very center of its paramour's life. Leo is vivacious and giving; Taurus tends to be sober and selfish. There will be little to complain about in the sexual area, but Leo must set the mood and pace. Hard-to-please Leo may prove troublesome in an affair, and for the long pull this is not a good combination.

TAURUS and VIRGO: Taurus is more physical and may be bothered by Virgo's tilt toward the puritanical. In lovemaking, Virgo prefers the simple way and not too much frenzy if you please. Taurus doesn't mind the simple way, but its relentless approach to sex may cause Virgo some disquiet. Otherwise, not too many problems between them. A good affair; a marriage should work, but may depend on sexual compromise.

TAURUS and LIBRA: Libra will bring to their sex life a good deal of emotional warmth and the concentration necessary to analyze and solve any physical problems. Libra will make the extra effort to titillate and satisfy. Taurus is also persistent, so the odds are good for mutual fulfillment in this area. Taurus can take the lead in the bedroom. A *simpatico* affair and probably a good bet for a more permanent union.

TAURUS and SCORPIO: They have a considerable sexual appetite in common. Also, neither feels any particular need for outside affairs. If angered, Taurus can be stubborn and Scorpio's own anger, when roused, is something of which all signs of the zodiac should beware. A tempestuous affair is indicated, and marriage is possible only with extreme tolerance.

TAURUS and SAGITTARIUS: The danger here is that Taurus will try to tie a string to independent Sagittarius. That can't work. Highly sexed Taurus will be pleased by Sagittarius's lustiness but annoyed by its compulsion to seek love wherever it can be found. They will have fun together, but happy-go-lucky Sagittarius is usually a much better lover than mate.

TAURUS and CAPRICORN: Equally strong sexual desires are at work. Neither wants unrestrained unconventional sex. Taurus won't like Capricorn's native secrecy about what it expects. And Capricorn won't like Taurus's attempts to take what it wants. There won't be much "romance" between these two, but they can have a sensual amour or a very good long-term partnership.

TAURUS and AQUARIUS: Introspective Aquarius isn't as interested as Taurus in the physical aspects of love. Aquarius would prefer to commune on a mental plane, but that kind of love won't satisfy passionate Taurus. Aquarius, in turn, may feel Taurus is too demanding. However, Aquarius likes to explore erotic techniques and might be intrigued in this way. A casual affair, an unpromising marriage.

TAURUS and PISCES: Pisces has a volatile, unpredictable temperament in a sexual encounter. Taurus may find this hard to handle. By helping Pisces to act out its fantasies and by tactful and firm encouragement, a determined Taurus can increase Pisces' receptiveness. The success of the sexual arrangement depends on Taurus. There are good prospects for an ardent affair and for a satisfactory marriage.

GEMINI

May 21–June 20

THE FEMALE

She's a one-girl harem. Ten women would be hard put to it to match her virtuosity. Like a genie in a bottle, each time you summon her up an entirely different woman will appear to mystify, delight, beguile, and enchant you.

She can fix and hold the attention of almost anyone, for she is a delightful conversationalist, witty, provocative, charming. She is also a sympathetic listener who will become very interested in your problems. Tell her your ambitions, your desires, your fears and prepare yourself for answers. Some think it presumptuous to try to solve other people's problems by offering *their* solutions. Not Gemini, who loves to analyze situations, dissect motivations, offer advice.

She makes friends easily, but is not usually interested in a long-term, more demanding relationship. She will devote a great deal of time and attention to keeping her friends happy. Depend on her for the quick charming note, the timely telephone call, the apt compliment. She will wear her heart on her sleeve for any friend to see—but for none to possess.

She wants everyone to like her, although she does not necessarily like everyone. Basically, she resents it if someone takes too much of her time or continues to burden her with a problem that she has already solved—to her satisfaction.

She continually seeks new outlets for her abundant energy and exuberance. She will go anywhere on a moment's notice without weighing the pros and cons, and she will often make important decisions on the same quicksilver basis. She tends to rely on her reflexes rather than her judgment.

She finds it rather hard to stick to one task because her interests are always straying to the next. Nothing fascinates her more than novelty. As a result, she often feels that she is disorganized. She vows to follow through one job from beginning to the end and may honestly try. She can't. As soon as she gets to the mid-way point, she begins champing at the bit, eager to turn down that undiscovered path that seems to promise so much more in the way of excitement.

Highly emotional, she can run through the gamut from A to Z in the same time that others travel from A to B. It's as difficult for her to commit herself to a single emotion as it is to commit herself to a single lover, a single job, or a single plan.

A bewildering and complex woman, a gay and lovely comrade, a vivacious life-enhancer—she is also subject to dark moods of self-doubt, an absolute terror of the unknown. That's when she needs a strong shoulder to lean on.

Although she is warm and affectionate, there are many who regard her as cold blooded. That's because she tends to rely on intelligence rather than emotions. Gemini is ruled by Mercury, planet of the mind. You must meet her on her own high intellectual level.

Don't try to tie her down. She's a free spirit, not a bird for anyone's gilded cage. Nothing lifts her spirits more than to arrive at a place she likes or to leave one she doesn't. That applies to her relationships with people as well as places.

She demands mental compatibility in a sexual partner and will not be relegated to an inferior position. As a result, she tends to make a better career woman than housewife. If she chooses, she can do both jobs well. But if she's forced to do both, she will quickly rebel.

She is prone to become involved with many men, particularly in her youth. Usually she is not content to devote herself to remaking and rearranging the life and character and career of only *one* man.

She is also constantly changing and rearranging, redecorating, looking for a new place to live, trying new foods, new fad diets, new amusements—never quite content with the way things are. When not working on herself and her immediate surroundings, she will be working on her lover—trying to improve him. Perhaps this helps to explain why so many attractive Gemini women remain single. There is nothing she can do about this trait, so her man must learn to put up with it. Change is part of her life pattern—the one thing she *can't* change!

She likes luxury and will try hard to attain it. That includes using her sex appeal. Because she is so detached emotionally, it's easy for her to use sex as a weapon. And she has all the charm and imagination needed to make the weapon work for her.

In her relations with men, she often plays what appears to be a heartless game. But an abused lover is usually willing to forgive and forget—if she'll take him back.

Those who can keep up with her will find the experience most rewarding. After all, where else can you find a woman who makes your life half as interesting? She's entrancing, exasperating—and all woman.

HER SEX LIFE

She needs no special setting or locale. The back seat of a car at the local drive-in movie or even a balcony seat in the local movie theater is perfectly adequate. Her main requirement is a lover who knows how to take enough time. For she won't be rushed.

Her lovemaking mood can change with startling abruptness—particularly if the man comes on too strong. She wants to establish her own rate of progress, and woe betide the lover who tries to speed matters to a quick conclusion. She can turn on enough refrigeration to chill the ardor in any man's veins.

Allow the right mood to develop, until the oneness of desire unites you. She enjoys the whole gamut from verbal byplay to titillation, from sensual excitement to lasciviousness. She will repay your patience with her own brand of sexual exuberance—and that's all any man could ask for!

But a lover who wants to keep her interest longer should be aware that, apart from the basic sexual urge, Gemini is looking for an ideal. A relationship for her has to be an embracing communion that includes the physical and the spiritual, the romantic and the practical.

She is often the aggressor. Recent studies have shown that the sexually aggressive female doesn't turn off men. Men are usually grateful for overt and explicit advances. Take a Gemini woman boating on the lake, and she may quickly indicate that she'd prefer you to put your own oar in. Take her on a picnic for two, and she may bring along a nice cuddly blanket and a pillow. After all, there's no sense eating on the hard cold ground!

She can be quick tinder. As with men born under this sign, it is not a need for sex or even the pleasurable sensations derived from it that provides the motivation. She is simply curious. And she is never embarrassed by her behavior, because she never adheres to any standard but her own.

One Gemini woman, about forty and not particularly attractive, told me her method for stirring a cloddish lover's libido. She chooses a nice private corner table in a dimly lit bar, unzips his fly while they are having drinks, masturbates him, and catches his semen in her half-empty liquor glass. Then while he's pulling himself together, she twirls the glass gently and slowly finishes her drink. That's a message no man has ever failed to get—or remember!

Gemini always likes to do two things at one time. In foreplay, she will combine deep kissing with manual stimulation of other erogenous zones. While performing fellatio, she will tantalize a lover with a delicate finger massage on the abdomen or by seizing a buttock in each hand to lift and pull in time with her oral manipulations. She has good intuitions about lovemaking and devises many delightful and daringly different variations.

One lovely Gemini woman I know only enjoys building up to sex with the aid of fine French champagne. She takes a lover into the bathtub and uncorks a bottle of the bubbly. The spray directed at the genital area excites them both. She showers her lover with the rest of the bottle, letting the liquid drip in little rivulets down the thighs. Then she laps it up and up—and up.

The Gemini female is always seeking more satisfaction from sex. Impelled by her restless imagination, her endless curiosity, she has intercourse more frequently than women born under other signs and tries various kinds of far-out experimentation. She is frequently bisexual (that duality again!), and in love affairs with members of her own sex prefers to alternate taking the woman's or the man's role.

In making love with a male partner, she is sometimes inclined toward the sadistic. She will practice such delights as squeezing a man's testicles while copulating, leaving him torn between exquisite pain and exquisite pleasure.

In her search for ultimate ecstasy, she is also drawn to fetishes. She can be aroused quite easily by body odors, that of a woman menstruating or a man perspiring heavily, the damp emanation from his testicles or the faint odors from his soiled shorts. The full range of fetishes is her range, but she is more physically than emotionally excited by them. Curiosity, not real kinkiness, is the name of her game.

Like male Gemini, she is interested in sex gimmicks. One of her favorites is the twin golden balls. She inserts the two small balls deep into her vagina and then, lying on her stomach or bending over a chair, is entered from the rear by the male. While he pushes in and out gently, the massaging motion of the gold balls impels her to orgasm after orgasm. Why gold, or at least gold-painted balls? Well, Gemini likes luxury—and if she wants to be her own kind of ball-buster, why argue?

THE MALE

He is always in transit—from one place to another, one person to another, one vocation to another. Restless, nervous, he is not content to live one day at a time, but will try to compress a week or a month into a day and to live on several different levels at once.

Whatever he is doing at the moment, he yearns to do something else. He thrives on contradiction. You can't even be sure when he likes you, for his mode of expression is always so contradictory. If he doesn't seem to know you're alive, he's probably intensely aware of your existence. If he is overly solicitous and attentive, he probably couldn't care less. Whatever his feeling, his first instinct is to camouflage it.

He can't stand schedules. Don't ask him to have all his meals at set hours or even to maintain regular hours for going to sleep or waking. He won't be a prisoner to the clock.

He is unusually intelligent and has a clever gift of gab. And how he loves to talk! He will juggle several topics, keeping them all in the air at the same time.

Don't try to win a verbal battle with him. He is highly articulate, and words are weapons he can wield with devastating effect.

A strange restlessness is evident even in his conversation, for he jumps from topic to topic like Eliza crossing the ice. He is free flowing, spontaneous, and highly volatile. This gives an impression of electric magnetism rather than lack of control, because what he is saying sparkles with a special glitter and radiance. He is a fascinating, many-sided, intellectual man, constantly and almost painfully aware of how people react to him.

His enthusiasm results in his tackling too many enterprises and spreading himself too thin. He will display great initiative in launching a project. The problem is to keep him on course. All too often, quick-witted Gemini is left behind by plodding, less imaginative competitors, for he is notoriously the da Vinci of dilettantes.

He doesn't react well to failure. He is all too eager to blame himself, to trigger depressed emotions in which the failure confirms his secret feelings of inadequacy. However, these moods don't last long. Some new interest comes along to intrigue him and sends his emotional chart zooming upward again.

He's interested in games, hobbies, all manner of diversion. He loves to travel, in order, as one Gemini male put it, "to see sights these eyes have never seen before." He is a hard worker, but only for a short stretch. And he does best at any kind of work that presents a stimulating mental challenge. He needs frequent intervals, vacations, breaks in routine. Fundamentally, he is much more interested in hobbies and recreation than in work of any kind.

He loves being in love and will try to take it where-ever he can find it. But he also seeks his freedom and will not submerge his ego to please any woman. He is also easily bored by routine, and when subjected to it is likely to become hostile and seek out quarrels. He always must establish his intellectual superiority. If a woman accepts this too easily, he will be frustrated. There has to be some resistance, some protest or struggle, before he is satisfied with his victory.

His biggest problem: making up his mind. Because

he finds it difficult to stick to one course or to pursue anything to a conclusion, he is accused of being fickle and contradictory. Once the main thrust of a challenge has been met, he immediately begins looking for something new, different—just over the horizon . . .

That's also true of his behavior in the business world. Usually, he will be regarded as the brightest of executives, a truly brilliant idea man, well qualified to find his place at the top. But he won't hang around the company long enough to gain the eminence for which his talents suit him. He'll blitz a problem, deploying all his resources and all the skills of those who work for him. Traditional practices or business dogma won't stand in his way, for he has no patience with the old way of doing things. It will only be a comparatively short time, however, before people discover he also has no patience with the new way of doing things. He'll be looking for something still more advanced. Finally he'll run into too much opposition and simply pack up and move on. His best role is as a troubleshooter or business consultant, where the steady stream of new problems will keep him engrossed, and he won't have to bother himself with seeing to it that his orders are carried out. Gemini male likes to plan the strategy and leave the day-to-day tactics to others.

He has difficulty holding on to money. Possessions slip through his grasp. When he has too much money in the bank, he is uncomfortable and tries to discover a reason to rid himself of it. He finds security only in insecurity.

Many people think he has captured the spirit of youth, with its endless vitality and curiosity, its love of fun and partying, even of movies and TV. He is called the Peter Pan of the zodiac because he never seems to grow up.

Women are not the most important thing in his life —although he gets more than his share. Often known as a chaser, it is not because he is oversexed but simply because he loves to sample new wares. At the beginning of an affair he is marvelous, everything a woman could ask for, but his emotional charge is soon spent—and will probably need recharging by someone new and different. His emotions are often shallow. The future with him is uncertain; the present is undeniably fun.

HIS SEX LIFE

You won't find him breathing heavily. He isn't demanding or passionate. He plays a dual role—the one making love and the one watching, participant and voyeur. If he chooses, he can work any partner into the mood, for he knows exactly how to evoke the right responses.

The idea rather than the act attracts him; not so much the pleasure derived from sexual activity as what psychologists call apperception—the ability to perceive *how* he is perceiving. Thus, while doing, he is also satisfying his inquisitiveness as to how it is being done; while reacting he is studying how he is reacting. He is always both the doer and the onlooker.

He prefers sex with the lights on, and one of his favorite stimuli is to have mirrors set up so he can see the action duplicated from every angle. One Gemini male correspondent told me that he particularly likes to screen stag movies while copulating. He will then either emulate the action on the screen or experiment with his partner in an attempt to go beyond it.

He warms up gradually. Cunnilingus isn't especially his forte and he isn't turned on by fellatio, but he enjoys the other preliminaries. He can dally delightfully, nibbling your ears, lightly raking your back with his fingernails, artfully playing the game of sexual arousal before moving on to his goal. Coitus is likely to be fast and furious. Gemini, even when he has had what he wants, is of two minds as to whether it was really worthwhile.

He likes to make love just about anywhere and is glib enough to talk his way into almost any woman's bed. But his performance rating is only fair, for he tends to be more interested in satisfying himself, or his curiosity, than his partner. Not too many women complain, even if they sometimes suspect they are mere grist to the mill of his experience, for he is more than adequate in the areas of lovemaking that are so often neglected by other males. He tells a woman exactly what she wants to hear, creates a special aura of excitement and romance, and that, more than sheer physical excitement, makes her look forward to a return match.

Warning: Even if he convinces you of his absolute sincerity, don't put too much faith in it. He is a Pied Piper who will be off to lead another victim to follow his winning tune. His sincerity is "real"—but only in the sense that he means what he says *when* he says it.

Group sex is a particular favorite, including bisexual activity, for he enjoys the multiple and varied opportunities it affords. Variety really is the spice of his life. A favorite variant is for him to make love to one partner while another masturbates in front of him.

A Gemini friend tells me he gets his most erotic kicks while skindiving. He and his partner come together twenty feet below the surface. He is excited by the concentration needed to have sex while continuing to keep his breathing even and regular as required for skindiving. He calls it "aquafucking!"—an ultimate thrill.

Gemini is intrigued by gadgets. He will experiment with hard-on pills, penis extenders, sprays to deaden nerves and delay ejaculation, and so-called orgy oils. Among Gemini male acquaintances, I count one who owns a battery-operated rubber penis that rotates, buzzes, or wriggles, another who habitually employs a double-pronged dildo with which he excites a woman at both ends while he is himself being fellated, and another who has a vibrator kit that has many different sleeves to excite and exhilarate all parts of the body. Trust a Gemini male to seek out anything that will promise to add more excitement!

Because he is pulled in two directions (the sign of the Twins, remember), he has a tendency toward bisexuality. Some, while retaining their heterosexual status, become transvestites, satisfying duality of desire by wearing a woman's clothes and makeup. A recent letter from a Gemini male correspondent told me how he had bought an artificial vagina in order to "really experience" the sensation of being a woman. (I'm sure that the experience lacked at least one necessary ingredient.) However, the letter was interesting in its revelation of both the divided nature and the curiosity of the typical Gemini male.

His quest for more and more unusual forms of gratification inclines him toward violent forms of sadism in which there is always a clearly delineated master and slave relationship. Male Gemini is strongly attracted to prostitutes of the cheapest kind, who will do anything to satisfy a customer's bizarre taste for experiment. You can be sure Dr. Jekyll was a Gemini, for the celebrated duality of his nature that turned him into Mr. Hyde, the curiosity exemplified in his far-out scientific experiments, and his violent and degrading treatment of his lower-class mistress are all classic instances of Gemini behavior.

FIRST MOVES

In the first minute you'll feel as if you've known Gemini forever. Conversation overflows with ideas, witticisms, interesting experiences. You're laughing before you know it. Life seems much more exciting than just before you met.

I try to have two Gemini people at any party because then I don't worry about its being a success. Gemini won't allow a group to slide off into apathy. Their vibrant magnetism can light up a room like a pinwheel of lights, and they treat boredom like a personal enemy.

It's always best to keep Gemini guessing. They are piqued by uncertainty. Try making a date in which he or she won't know where you're going until you get there. And make sure it isn't too disappointing when you do! Wining and dining with Gemini is never enough; it should be a new or unusual place. It needn't be expensive (though Gemini won't mind that), but it definitely has to be different.

Be alert and lively if you want to attract Gemini to you. Don't let on too soon that you are fascinated by them. They prefer a little mystery and are tantalized by those who hold something in reserve, indicating that they have secret depths or undisclosed meanings. Remember: Gemini is eternally curious.

The key word is imagination. Take him or her to that really exceptional party where celebrities are guests or where brilliant conversation or fun games will be played. If all else fails, try a masquerade party. The ingenuity required to create a really striking costume will intrigue Gemini.

Don't pass up daytime events such as art museums—especially private showings—afternoon concerts or library exhibits. Gemini is an intellectual!

On a date avoid the routine neighborhood movie or restaurant. Go roller-skating or to a roller derby, play miniature golf, watch a lacrosse match, attend an offbeat lecture on yoga. Introduce Gemini to those "socially awkward" friends whose genuine qualities no one has ever been able to bring out. Gemini will soon have them displaying facets of their character and revealing things about their background that not even you suspected.

Let Gemini do the talking. They are spontaneous self-starters, and all you have to be is a good listener. Wear them out with listening, and they'll talk themselves into falling in love with you.

When you're going out, try to put that celebrated Gemini duality to work for you. Never plan a dinner or a movie. Plan both. If Gemini male can't afford to pick up a dinner check, suggest ice cream afterward or a late snack and coffee. When you're talking about the movie you've just seen (or whatever), don't be reluctant to begin a few amorous preliminaries. Geminis of both sexes know how to keep two interesting activities going at one and the same time!

By all means, cultivate their family. Be agreeable if they suggest an evening watching home movies or if they trot out the family album of photographs. You can always turn on the hi-fi. Gemini won't mind, for they can pay attention to both.

If you have extremist or fanatical convictions in either religion or politics, you won't get along well with Gemini. They see everybody's side of the question all too clearly. They are liberal and tolerant by nature, and narrowminded people won't get far with them.

Geminis love to gossip, so save up what juicy tidbits you read in newspapers or magazines or hear about friends and acquaintances. They will weigh in with some occasional scathing comments, especially in the sphere of morality, but don't take that seriously. It isn't a clue to how Gemini will behave when you pop the proposition to her or let him know you're willing to hear him pop it. They hold one set of opinions about others' behavior and an entirely different one about their own.

Don't expect them not to kiss and tell, however. They will.

EROGENOUS ZONES

The hands and arms up to the shoulder are especially sensitive areas. Gemini women are responsive to hand-kissers; Gemini men like to have their fingers sucked slowly, one at a time.

For either sex, try running your hand lightly over Gemini's arm. Barely touching the skin will raise goosebumps—almost as if the nerve endings were attempting to touch *you* back. The accidental caress of fingertips on a hand can send shivers of delight up their spines. Kissing on the inside of their arms is a special treat. For an interesting (and provocative) variation, move your lips and tongue lightly from the elbow to the armpit. You can practically sense the signals of desire flashing.

LAST MOVES

How to break off the affair? Simple. The method can be summed up under one heading: Be boring. Don't communicate. When you do, tell long-winded stories in exhaustive detail. Gemini will listen with the look of someone drowning in a vat of peanut butter.

Discuss controversial subjects. Gemini hates quarrels. And while you're about it, don't let Gemini get a word in edgewise.

Tell your problems in tiresome detail. Gemini finds other people's problems depressing.

Be impatient and temperamental. They can't stand it.

Always go to the same places, see the same people, do the same things, tell the same jokes.

When you make love, do it in the same way, even in the same place. Don't change any of the preliminaries. By all means, talk about it at length afterward.

Take the dark view of everything. Gemini is a supreme optimist. Let them know that no matter how bad you think today is, tomorrow will get worse.

Restrict their freedom of movement. In fact, invent reasons for staying home night after night. Insist on help with housework—particularly the dullest chores. Have your most boring friends over for the most inane evening you can endure.

When the last guest leaves, Gemini will be leaving too—never to return.

YOUR SENSUAL GUIDE

GEMINI and ARIES: Both are lively, enthusiastic, and enjoy variety in their sexual relations. They won't easily become bored in the bedroom. Aries can give Gemini the firm direction it needs. Aries is stimulated rather than irritated by Gemini's occasional waywardness. An excellent match for a short-term liaison, with a good chance to develop into an affectionate long-term alliance.

GEMINI and TAURUS: Jealous, possessive Taurus can't take flirtatious Gemini. Gemini resents and will try to escape from Taurus's restrictive net. Sexually, Taurus is too dull for Gemini who, in turn, cannot give Taurus the security this sign needs. If this sounds like the two signs are not compatible, you're right. An unhappy short-lived affair is the most likely result.

GEMINI and GEMINI: This might be a lot of fun while it lasts, but it will very quickly become unstable.

Except for a transient physical attraction, all signposts indicate the direct route to chaos. Both are flirtatious, impulsive, easily bored. The course of love will be turbulent and the marriage a probable disaster. In rare instances where this combination does work, however, they're the most interesting couple you know.

GEMINI and CANCER: Danger ahead for this pairing. Cancer is too sensitive and shy to reveal its true feelings. Gemini will play at love while Cancer takes it seriously. Cancer needs praise and reassurance, while Gemini can be too cruelly frank. These temperamental differences will be a frequent source of trouble in the bedchamber. An affair runs steadily downhill, a marriage will eventually founder.

GEMINI and LEO: Big-hearted, generous Leo is silly putty in the hands of Gemini—and loves it! Gemini is versatile and clever in sexual play, and Leo will respond with admiration and affection. Leo is content to let Gemini pursue its own way without carping or suspicion. An ideal mating. There will be excitement and fun in an affair, and the auguries are also bright for a more permanent relationship.

GEMINI and VIRGO: Virgo considers Gemini an immature lover; Gemini considers Virgo a stick-in-the-mud and a bore. Virgo has fixed opinions about sexual conduct; Gemini vacillates. After the fires of passion burn low, Virgo will tend to nag and criticize Gemini, and Gemini will turn a roving eye elsewhere in search of variety. A pair of star-crossed lovers who shouldn't count on a long future.

GEMINI and LIBRA: An attractive, interesting pairing. Both are affectionate, and their lovemaking is likely to become fervent. Neither is jealous or possessive, and their temperaments interact to stabilize each other. Both are willing to experiment with sex. They should enjoy an affair. In marriage, especially if Libra can convince Gemini to watch the pocketbook, they have an excellent chance for happiness.

GEMINI and SCORPIO: Sexually compatible, but these two prove that raw physical attraction isn't everything. Scorpio is jealous, Gemini is fickle. When Scorpio pulls the reins too tight, Gemini will kick over the traces. After a passionate interlude, an affair will quickly cool into unpleasantness and even hostility. In marriage, only an exceptional pair will make a go of it.

GEMINI and SAGITTARIUS: Both are restless, changeable, and not too demonstrative as lovers. Gemini will tend to criticize Sagittarius's performance beneath the bedcovers. There are other weak points in this relationship but a source of strength is the fact that neither is demanding or possessive. An affair will begin impulsively and end the same way. Both have to work at a marriage, but if they do it can be rewarding.

GEMINI and CAPRICORN: Gemini is too free-wheeling, impatient, and independent for conservative, steady, home-loving Capricorn. Some of Gemini's sexual behavior will prove embarrassing to staid Capricorn. Capricorn worries about more than its physical needs —job, money, career—and thinks Gemini scatterbrained. An affair is possible, but a successful marriage between these two is proof of love conquering all.

GEMINI and AQUARIUS: Sensitive Gemini understands and appreciates the fantasies of Aquarius. They can become adventurous, inventive lovers. The hallmark of the relationship will be its unpredictability. Amour may not always run smooth, but can be exciting and rewarding. When the affair is over, they'll remain friends. Marriage is likely to be comfortable and pleasant, marked by deep affection rather than passion.

GEMINI and PISCES: They will be better at thinking up new sexual schemes than at carrying them out. Pisces is a bit too emotional for Gemini, whose impulse is to enjoy the experience—and move on. This tends to breed an atmosphere of suspicion and mistrust. There can be real affection between these two, but eventually the insecurity will erode the relationship. A somewhat risky affair, an unhappy marriage.

CANCER

June 21–July 22

THE FEMALE

You need a compass to travel around this lunar lady's emotional landscape. If you don't have the right compass, you'll be totally lost in determining where you are with her.

When in doubt, remember this rule: She is very dependent on the support of those close to her, although too shy to express what she feels. And she has an absolute horror of criticism, particularly of ridicule. Nothing wounds her more or seems more cruel and unjust. Her tenacious memory clings to the hurtful memory until she has a chance to wreak revenge.

Speaking of memory, hers is an engraving on a steel plate. Almost nothing can erase it. She will continually astonish you with snippets of recall from previous conversations and meetings. I know one woman born under this sign who can remember almost every line of dialogue from her favorite movies. Even if she hasn't seen the movie for years, she will recite the lines an actor is going to speak before he says them.

One reason for Cancer woman's retentiveness is that she treasures the past. She would prefer to live there if it were possible, and if she has any belief in the occult she may actually think she did live there in some previous incarnation. She likes to read history, particularly about the last fifty to a hundred years—and will furnish her home with antiques of that period. She likes framed portraits of elegant ladies in turn-of-the-century gowns, for such mementoes of an earlier era provide her with a secure sense of continuity. Life for her is never merely the here and now.

She loves her home and will spend delightful hours in furnishing it to her taste. Her decorative sense tends to be a little old-fashioned, but it is never dowdy. Her kitchen is as warm and inviting as one in an old Dutch painting. For her there truly is no place like home, although she has no intention of letting it be ever so humble.

No one goes hungry in this woman's domain. She's a great cook. Her refrigerator is stuffed to the bulging point with provisions and goodies. That's part of her overriding desire for security. She simply must know where her next meal is coming from—and her next dollar. Almost the first thing she learned about money matters is that it does.

She isn't a miser, but she will put money away against a rainy, sunny, warm, cold day—with a little extra in case a hurricane should strike. The only time she'll willingly part with cash is to use it as a balm for her bruised spirit. Some emotional traumas can be healed by a spending spree, but even then she tends to spree on the kind of items, like diamonds, that have a redeemable value in trustworthy coin of the realm.

She is not a gossip. Tell her almost anything without fear of it being passed on. Where other people's confidences are concerned, she is virtually a grave of secrecy.

She is a marvelous story teller of another kind though. Listen to her on an evening with close friends when she begins to loosen up and tell anecdotes—probably out of her own past or her family's. She controls the mood of her listeners with just a slight alteration in tone, a change of nuance in the phrasing, and the word imagery with which she spins her tale would do credit to Nathaniel Hawthorne. One slight exception—she can't tell a funny story without giggling. When something strikes her as funny, the reaction begins and bubbles up to her lips. Sometimes—usually when someone else has amused her—it will break out into an open laugh. Her laugh is not her best feature. It has a silly, or semi-hysterical, quality, the kind that used to be referred to as "looney"—for good reason, since that refers to the lunar influence, and the Moon just happens to be her ruler!

She is loyal to friends and to the man she chooses to be her mate. Sometimes her loyalty takes on a clinging quality. In turn, she expects almost constant affection from her lover. She needs to be fussed over, snuggled, prized, doted on. She must be wooed with tender care and patient consideration, for she will retreat from an aggressive man.

It is difficult for her to give herself in love, although she is very attractive to men because of her modesty, winsomeness, and sympathetic understanding of their personal problems. She is that shy, sweet, lovely girl in white organdy whose image every man carries in a secret locket somewhere in his mind. If you want to win her, don't overlook the roses, candlelight, champagne, and love sonnets. This is not going to be a quickie conquest. In fact, it will more likely develop to where it's all or nothing, live or die, marry or part forever. Weigh your decision carefully. If you lose her, she will always be a vagrant, haunting memory.

There are two things this woman must have in combination—love and security. She reaches for the kind of love that is more than sex—that means home, children, and a stable relationship. You won't get into her bedroom until she's sure of your long-term intentions. She may be feminine, but she's no man's fool.

When she finds real love, she will go all out for her mate, and she is fully capable of becoming the most satisfying sex partner in the zodiac! Her sincerity in the act of love makes her the worst possible candidate in any "play for pay" arrangement—whether as a prostitute, call girl, or simply a marriage arranged for material reasons. She can't fake a sexual response.

However, in the right circumstances, she *can* be a devoted mistress, provided she knows the man is truly unable to marry her or that he is genuine in his belief that marriage does not matter. She is passionately loyal once she has committed herself to a man. Any man who wins her for a mistress would be well advised to make her a wife—just to make sure he doesn't lose this treasure!

Not that he has to worry much about losing her. She is the prototype for the song "Stand by Your Man." She will stand by him even though he's an alcoholic, a bully, or a not-so-secret swinger. Some men complain that this kind of all-forgiving love can be smothering, and psychiatrists look for an explanation in her unconscious fear that she is unworthy and therefore cannot demand fair treatment in love.

Whatever the reason, Cancer women are often mistreated by men.

HER SEX LIFE

Although she is receptive, she will never make the first move. She is much too shy, and she is also afraid that if she emerges too far from her shell, she will meet with criticism. She has to be encouraged in the subtlest way until her erotic imagination is freed of its inhibitions. She has to be shown that she can act in love as she really feels, respond with the kind of actions that will strongly excite a man, and not fear the promptings of her own libido.

Her sensitive nature is much influenced by the attitude of her partner. If he is understanding, sympathetic, kind, considerate, she will unfold to him as a flower does to the warming rays of the sun. But it is all too easy to frighten her into a shy and secretive retirement with a harsh word or a wrong gesture or expression. The shell of her self-confidence cracks too easily.

She can be a marvelous lover, for she is capable of intense sensuality. The joy she feels on the release of previous restraints will delight any man. She will reciprocate passion with a fervor that will stir his heart and stimulate him to his best performance. She may even become a slave to sexual pleasure once she has achieved it.

During the early stages of lovemaking, try to appeal to her strong maternal and sentimental side, for this will heighten and deepen the power of the subsequent sexual union.

However, always remember that with this woman the time and occasion also have to be right. Don't expect to make out in the back seat of a car. She must believe that you care, and you must be in a place where she's entirely comfortable.

Her own nest is best, for home is her terrain. (Your place will do only if she's been there often enough not to feel like a stranger.) In fact, when the big night arrives, she will probably invite you to dinner at her place. Count your lucky stars and forget to count calories. Dinner will be marvelous, and there will be candlelight and good music. Don't be too aggressive, though, or you may never get from the dining room into the bedroom.

When she takes off her clothes for the first time, she expects to be told how lovely she is. Cancer women dote on admiration. A compliment is fully as important as any other preliminary, and you know already that she isn't going to like being rushed. In love, unlike the racetrack, the race is not always to the swift.

When she begins to lose some of her inhibitions, she likes to see and fondle male genitalia and to let her lover's testicles dangle in the palm of her hand. She also inflicts love bites on the inside of the thigh, high up near the crotch.

Another ambiance that works is the beach at night, especially by the light of the silvery moon. The magnetic rays of her ruling satellite dazzle her, the pounding surf deafens her with nature's melody. She is apt to shed all her inhibitions and reveal a side of her nature you never knew existed—wanton and wild and wonderful.

The fully sensual Cancer woman likes to anoint her fingers with honey or wine and caress her mate's sex organ until it becomes a steeple. Her touch is as light and gentle as a leaf falling. Her fingers slowly climb the steeple until it quivers with ecstatic readiness. Sometimes she stops there and helps her partner to masturbate. Sometimes she will slowly suck off the honey or wine until climax occurs. Most often she will stop just short of completion in order to mount her lover and lead him on to orgasm.

Sometimes she heightens oral intercourse for the male with a flavored douche—or sometimes she insists that her partner coat his penis with some flavoring. For reasons I haven't been able to discover, lemon, lime, and strawberry are favorites to titillate her taste buds.

Favorite position: lying prone while the man enters her from behind. That satisfies her innate modesty—she doesn't have to be seen having an orgasm—and also pleases a latent Cancerian desire to rub her buttocks against the man.

Cancer women are moody, and when they don't feel like having conventional sex they are often quite inventive. One woman of my acquaintance, when indisposed, still satisfies her lover by taking a jar and stuffing it with rags that have been soaked in heavy olive oil or mineral oil to serve as an artificial vagina. So far, she tells me, no complaints!

Cancer females are not as a rule subject to extreme sexual variations. However, when they are, they are likeliest to show up as a facet of her strong maternal instinct. For example, she may turn to pedophelia and have intercourse with very young boys. They are also drawn toward incest. I recall an unhappy young Cancer woman, quite attractive, telling me that when her mother gave birth to a brother some eight years younger than she, her first thought on looking at him in the hospital nursery had been that now she had someone "built in" she could make love with. When she was twenty years old, she succeeded in achieving her long-suppressed desire.

Since many Cancer women feel men are too rough in their lovemaking, they are also occasionally drawn to their own sex. In lesbian affairs, they tend to take the female role.

In a further reaction to male "roughness," some Cancer women prefer masturbation. When a dildo is not available, they are practical enough to use whatever artificial aid is—the sausage, the cucumber, or, in season, the banana.

THE MALE

You won't read him like an open book, for he shows an opaque side to strangers. There are some secrets he never reveals, even to his closest friends.

He is restless, prone to brooding, idealistic, a day-dreamer who is also very sentimental. Because he is ruled by the waxing and waning Moon, he has marvelous emotional highs and abysmal lows—and the alarming ability to pull people along with him in either direction.

At first meeting he may appear to be fickle and flirtatious—but that's only one of his moods. He is strongly subject to the cyclical action of the Moon. The very next time you meet him he may be sullen, unfriendly.

After you get to know him, you may still find his swift alternation of moods bewildering. Opposed, he may flare into violence. But if you give in too easily, he'll be apologetic for having won the argument. He may believe in Women's Lib, but he is forced by his nature to be protective and tender toward the "weaker sex." He is courteous and gallant, a charmer of the old school.

He loves the company of beautiful women—especially if they are witty conversationalists. Who doesn't? you ask, but the difference is that Cancer male is also very attractive to such women. However, when he has wooed and won them, he quickly becomes possessive. The woman he loves will have difficulty living up to his expectations, for he expects far too much. It doesn't help that he tends to sulk and withdraw into his shell when disappointed rather than to say openly what is bothering him.

He enjoys good food and drink, but don't expect him to dress up for an occasion. He doesn't care about clothes. He still has that old college sweater and those ancient tennis slacks that he now has trouble fitting around his middle. There is none of the peacock in the Cancer male.

He loves to talk and is often quite eloquent. His words alone can make people willing to follow him anywhere, do anything he asks. His fantastic memory and nearly total recall stand him in excellent stead in discussion and argument. He has firm convictions, and all goes well as long as you do not oppose those convictions. If you do, he will not let go until he has persuaded you. If he suspects you're not completely convinced, he will revive the discussion at the first opportunity in order to bombard you with further reasons. The debate will end only when you yield, if only for the sake of peace and quiet.

But he knows how to listen as well as talk. One woman I know described her Cancer man as "practically opening his pores to listen." He is deeply sympathetic, always ready to help someone else with a problem.

His keen, analytical mind can slice through the

knottiest problem. This makes him adept in money matters. He spots a moneymaking opportunity quicker than a lizard can spot a fly. But he is interested only in the conventional, conservative, traditional ways of making his fortune. He won't take risks.

He is sensitive, insecure, and very sentimental, reluctant to part with old friends, old habits, or places he has become accustomed to living in. He will keep a friend forever. He calls up his childhood buddies and meets them for a friendly drink—even if they no longer have anything in common. He resists and fears change in his mode of life. He clings to memories, scattering family pictures throughout his living quarters, keeping old school mementoes. He broods over the times gone by; he holds on tenaciously to the past.

He always needs reassurance of your love.

Don't look for a once-over-lightly romance with this man. He takes amour far too seriously. What he wants from his beloved is mental and physical stimulation in about equal measure. Intensely loyal, he demands absolute loyalty in return. He believes in a lasting affection—the kind that looks on tempests and is never shaken. That's his prescription for peace of mind.

He is no gadabout. The pleasures of hearth and home are best for him. He thinks compatibility begins in the home and contentment grows in his own backyard. But he does have a tendency toward self-satisfaction that borders on smugness, and a blind spot about the one he loves. I know one Cancer male who actually encouraged his girl friend to go off on an overnight car trip with a very attractive man. She was going to visit her mother, and he saw no reason to worry. Much later, after he married her, he discovered that she had spent the night in a motel room with her driving companion. He was so disturbed that he went to a psychoanalyst, who could not convince him that he had in any way contributed to the "betrayal." He never forgave her, and shortly afterward they ended up in the divorce court.

Cancer male looks for a long-term or permanent relationship with a woman. Yet if a rupture does occur, he can move on to a new love, for he has the knack of establishing intimacy very quickly. However, anyone who has really touched his emotions will never be truly forgotten, no matter what happens later.

He is a complex individual, whose changing moods make life with him anything but easy—and anything but dull. His tenacity of purpose is a good omen for success, and his sensitivity and intellect make him a natural leader in politics, literature, and business.

Warning: Beware of him on those nights of the full moon.

HIS SEX LIFE

He needs constant encouragement. If he gets it, he will be a delightful swain. He enjoys playing the role of teacher, and a woman is wise to let him believe he is initiating her into the true mysteries of sex. He will take her step by step, explaining what he is doing, and why, and what she's supposed to be doing. Don't stop him along the way with any remark that indicates you know all about that or have done it before, or he will promptly retreat into his shell, perhaps to dream of all the wonderful things you might have done together.

He is both patient and aggressive, and you have to go far to beat a combination like that. From the first whispered suggestion, he knows exactly where he is going—even though he may get there by a less than direct route. Let him take command. You'll like the trip. After all, it's as much fun traveling to a place as arriving.

In the beginning of a love affair, avoid any crudeness or vulgarity. He prefers to idealize a partner, and any jarring act—even if temporarily aphrodisiac—undermines the chances for a long sexual relationship. As times goes on, he will become more realistic, more willing to accept the kind of behavior that at first offends his conventional nature. At all times, though, you must be on guard against a sudden return to inherent fastidiousness. If not dealt with sympathetically, this can result in a kind of emotional withdrawal—the crab scuttling back to a place of safety.

In foreplay his pace is deliberate and sure, for he's interested in making you happy as well as in satisfying his own need. Unlike men who think it is a proof of virility to treat their loved one with sexual contempt, he has the all important sensitivity to mood that marks the really accomplished amorist.

He prefers to begin intercourse somewhere other than in bed. Holding you in his arms, he may back up to a table or bureau and lift you gently up on it. There he'll move from manual stimulation to subtle penile foreplay. While you're straining to feel the fullness of his desire, he'll suddenly lift you in his arms, not breaking contact, and carry you into bed.

He is expert at clitoral manipulation. He has a special gift in this technique of foreplay. He prefers to perform with his fingers and not orally, but his touch is so finely sensitive that he literally has exquisite sensations at his fingertips.

A favorite technique is to put his penis between a woman's breasts, close enough to his partner's mouth so that she can flick her tongue over its tip. The combination massage by breasts and tongue increases his pleasure—and adds a good deal to the excitement of foreplay for her.

What aids Cancer in lovemaking is his superb power of recollection. He remembers everything he has ever done that has aroused a woman to passion.

As he carries those youthful experiences with him into adulthood, he adds many imaginative refinements.

Another favorite technique is the "no-hands" coupling. Lying naked next to a partner in bed, both with their hands clasped behind their backs, he fumbles and gropes into position—causing a good deal of sensual excitement in the process. The fun is heightened if all is performed in front of a mirror to reflect some of the erotic contortions. Sometimes a third party is involved, who binds the lovers' hands behind them to prevent any "cheating" and then watches the resulting action. Cancer enjoys the satisfaction of achieving really good intercourse—despite such obstacles.

Heterosexual Cancer male likes his women to wear lacy, frilly underthings. Those who go over the thin dividing line into what some people call abnormality display a fondness for wearing those garments themselves. They enjoy dressing as women and passing themselves off in public as women, and their mimetic skills and ability to gauge other people's reactions enable them to carry off the masquerade perfectly. I was taken in by one such an attractive poised "woman" who came to me for a consultation. Only when I was working up "her" chart did certain inconsistencies appear. Finally my suspicions were awakened by responses that simply didn't jibe with what the stars indicated. At that point, "she" broke down and admitted to being a man. What was not visible to me even on close inspection was perfectly apparent in the stars!

Of course, many transvestites are pederasts, and the Cancer transvestite is no exception. Homosexuals born under this sign make the greatest effort to achieve physical transformation into women, including surgical alteration.

It is well known that latent homosexual tendencies exist in clearly heterosexual types. Cancer male will often satisfy such a tendency by this method: He will ask the woman to part his buttocks and press her crotch so hard against him that her pelvic bone is pushed against his anus. A few vigorous movements in this position will be enough to bring him to orgasm.

Many men born under this sign are frotteurs. They enjoy rubbing themselves against the buttocks or crotches of strangers, and public conveyances offer them the best opportunity for satisfying this particular hang-up.

FIRST MOVES

A good opening move is to seek advice about a problem. Cancer is sympathetic and helpful to strangers, and a Cancerian's advice is always to be valued.

Warning: DON'T try the old gambit of "Haven't I seen you somewhere before?" Cancer has a remarkable memory and recalls every incident, places every face. This is definitely a no-no.

When you meet someone born under this sign, turn the conversation toward charities for children and child-care organizations. The Cancer female is very interested in children and has even been accused of trying to be mother to the world. If so, the Cancer male is trying to be the father.

Or try your luck at politics, particularly with the male of the species. If your boss in a large business enterprise is a Cancer man, a good way to get closer is to bring him some personal problem. He has a paternal view toward all his employees—and whether you can change paternal into something more interesting is strictly up to you.

On a date, try theater, art, cultural pursuits. Cancer responds to strongly melodic, romantic music. Try a concert featuring Tschaikovsky or Rachmaninoff, and Cancer will be silently in tune with celestial harmonies. Or when you go out to dinner, arrange for soft music in the background. Or a restaurant with a gypsy violinist. Music is the food of love, as the bard says.

They are attracted to water sports, so invite them for a day at the beach or to an aquacade. If you pick a private enough beach, or one where there are no laws against it, your Cancer companion will gladly join you in skinny dipping. This gives them the satisfaction of letting you—and anyone else in sight—admire their bodies.

Like to give her a gift? Try something that enhances the home: pictures or tapestries for the walls, leather-bound books, even fancy cooking utensils. For him: boxed gifts of cheeses or exotic packaged foods. Or an elegant sterling silver frame engraved with his initials. Cancerians are usually collectors and will prize anything you add to their collection. Small silver objects delight them.

Cultivate a Cancerian's family, especially the mother. Most people born under this sign are sentimental about M-O-T-H-E-R.

Never, *never* refer to other love affairs. Cancer people are not interested in those who were important in your life before they came on the scene.

General dating advice: Those born under this sign never like to be taken for granted. If he shows up in a new suit, notice it; if she's wearing new earrings, remark on them. And try to be especially careful about their well-known hypersensitivity. You can tell her the earrings really look lovely, and she may decide that means you didn't like the earrings she wore last time. You may tell him his suit makes him look much more athletic, and he'll think you're saying he's pretty scrawny. If this sort of thing crops up, try to mend matters before the injury burrows too deep.

If you want to cancel a date because you're not feeling well, don't do it. You'd be a fool not to let Cancer show their strong protective side. They are the towers of strength, the lighthouses in a fog that everyone needs when under the weather. Let him come over with fruit and flowers, with a new book to read to you, with a new record to play, or just to sit by you and hold your hand. Let her give you your medicines, take your temperature (orally), and feed you hot soup. Anyone who hasn't experienced the solicitous affection of the Cancerian for someone he or she cares about doesn't know the chief delight of becoming seriously involved with them. It's just another way of showing possessiveness, but take advantage of it without inquiring too deeply into the reasons.

Call it Moon magic.

EROGENOUS ZONES

One of the biggest turn-ons for both male and female born under this sign is soul kissing—deep kissing, with full use of the tongue and teeth. They have been known to kiss to orgasm!

However, the most sensitive area of the body are the breasts. Both sexes will respond to oral and manual stimulation of their nipples. Caresses of the underside of the breast with a soft finger pad or fingertip create the most urgent sensations of sexual desire. They also like the "winding" movement, when the nipple is held between thumb and forefinger and wound like a watch. Even late in foreplay, a gentle tugging at the breast or nipples will add to their pleasure.

A trick for the woman making love with a Cancer male: Run your hand over his chest, barely touching the skin. The hair on his body will seem to reach up to touch your fingers. If you keep doing it, he'll go wild!

LAST MOVES

When you want to call it Q-U-I-T-S, you have a problem. Cancer is hard to get rid of. They stick like chewing gum to the bottom of your shoe.

A brusque insensitive manner will send her scurrying, but if you try to push her too hard, she will simply dig in and hold on. The way she fights back is through nagging—and she has an uncommon gift for that. Far better to work in less obvious ways. She looks for and needs tenderness. Withhold it. Don't let her share in your life, but indicate that her role is merely to wait on you. If this causes her anxiety, as it will, offer her no reassurance. Be moody—this has a direct effect on her emotions.

With him, be dominating, make the social plans, become the prime mover in the family. Make indifferent meals, serve them while grumbling about how culinary matters are the least interesting thing in your life.

Criticize his bedroom approach, his sex technique. He has a secret feeling he's dull in that department, so let him know you think so too. Unforgivable!

Cancer needs affection. Turn it off. Cancer needs emotional support. Be unavailable or too busy. Cancer likes to give advice. Don't listen. Cancer likes old and elegant places. Go to the most plastic commercial joints you can find.

Above all, criticize. All Cancers suffer from feelings of inadequacy, and criticism exploits their weakness.

Tell mother-in-law jokes.

YOUR SENSUAL GUIDE

CANCER and ARIES: Aries is somewhat too adventurous a lover for Cancer, who tends to be more conventional —though strong sexual attraction may exist at first. In time, Aries may provoke Cancer's moody jealousy, and Cancer will be too easily hurt by Aries's biting tongue. Aries will also find Cancer's possessiveness oppressive. A difficult affair; a marriage headed for the rocks.

CANCER and TAURUS: Cancer brings sensitivity and imagination to this union. Both are passionate and don't need outside interests to keep them content. Taurus is able to understand Cancer's vacillations of mood and will help smooth over any problems that raise. If Taurus is attentive, Cancer will respond in kind. An appreciation of each other's needs augurs an enjoyable affair, a successful marriage.

CANCER and GEMINI: Cancer's basic insecurity will be aggravated by fickle, flirtatious, fun-loving Gemini. Gemini's unguided sexual energies present problems to Cancer, causing frustration and difficulties. Cancer will become quite jealous and will try to restrict Gemini's activities, and that only makes Gemini resentful. A highly emotional affair and a longer relationship that will founder over basic difference in temperaments.

CANCER and CANCER: They are really too much alike to be happy. There is an abundance of sensitivity on both sides with resulting emotional problems. Both try to lead in sexual encounters and that provokes frequent criticism and argument. Physically, though, they are attractive to each other, and an initial relationship may be quite sensual. A marriage will require more sympathy and mutual understanding to survive.

CANCER and LEO: Leo tends to be a stabilizer for Cancer's moods. Leo is also generous with its affections and that reassures moody, insecure Cancer. On the other hand, Leo requires a great deal of flattery and admiration—particularly for its sexual prowess—and must dominate. If Cancer yields and provides what Leo needs, this can be a passionate affair and a triumphant marriage.

CANCER and VIRGO: Virgo's practical, agreeable nature provides a sound basis for this relationship. Cancer is more emotional than reserved Virgo, but they can develop a really warm and affectionate feeling for each other. Sexually, they get along quite well, although the heavens don't light with celestial fires. The problem is that both are shy and retiring and need to make an effort to avoid dullness. A fine affair, probably a comfortable marriage.

CANCER and LIBRA: Libra finds difficulty in sympathizing with Cancer's brooding temperament. In turn, Cancer becomes insecure and anxious at Libra's detachment. Actually, Libra is rather attracted to Cancer's moods but simply prefers to avoid trouble. If Cancer's affectionate nature is offended, it will lead to difficulties. When Libra begins to look elsewhere, the finish line is at hand. A possible affair, a risky marriage.

CANCER and SCORPIO: Scorpio's strength and need to dominate and protect are just what Cancer is looking for. Cancer is more sensitive in sex relations and

Scorpio, more passionate. But Cancer's desire to please helps to avoid any major problems in this area. Scorpio's fierce jealousy remains quiet, for Cancer is loyal to its mate. Love tends to deepen, and a fine affair can grow into a very good marriage.

CANCER and SAGITTARIUS: These two have opposite goals and different desires. Sagittarius is a rover and does not like to be fettered by sexual ties. Cancer needs the security in love that Sagittarius cannot offer. Cancer lives for the future, Sagittarius for the here and now. When Sagittarius becomes bored and begins to hanker for new horizons, Cancer will be hurt and embittered. Dim prospects for any workable liason.

CANCER and CAPRICORN: Capricorn can't come up with all the affection Cancer requires, for it has too many other interests. However, there is a strong sexual attraction between these two signs. They will have an interesting bedroom relationship until Capricorn's practicality and reserve begin to look like rebuffs to Cancer. An affair marked by instability; an unpromising marriage.

CANCER and AQUARIUS: Lone-wolf Aquarius deals too many bruises to Cancer's vulnerable ego. Cancer is more demonstrative and steadfast than adventurous Aquarius, who is always ready to heed siren calls. Cancer's needs may go unsatisfied, as Aquarius tends to absent itself from emotional demands. They may get along in the bedroom for a time, but the partnership will break down in the living room.

CANCER and PISCES: Sexually, this is a good match. Both are highly affectionate, responsive, and provide needed ego bolstering to each other. Cancer will probably take the lead, for Pisces tends to be somewhat oversubtle and eccentric in lovemaking. No quarrels will last long; most will be resolved quickly in bed. A compatible couple who can have great days —and nights—over the short or long haul.

LEO

July 23–August 22

THE FEMALE

She is always on display—a beautiful jewel in a shop window where all who pass stop to marvel. At an important social occasion she will be the most glittering female ornament. Even if she is temporarily in the wings, she feels like the star of a play waiting for the cue that summons her to center stage before an admiring audience.

To her, nothing is more important than that men admire and desire her. Her own feelings do not always become involved. In a sense she offers sex for sale, but her payment is only the satisfaction of knowing how dearly she is prized.

She not only has to be important to her mate, she has to be the one and only. That limitation, however, does not apply to her. She wants to be free to roam at will and find her prey. Usually she doesn't have to look far. The prey is all too willing. Leo women are the most popular huntresses in the veldt.

She likes people but is self-centered. She is domineering but dignified, vain but kind—a creature of contradictions who sees other people's problems only in relation to herself.

She is impetuous, unpredictable, alluring. Her emotions tend to be on the surface, with few depths. She is often "in love," rarely able to "love." She lacks the givingness of spirit, the ability to surrender herself to another person.

If a love affair becomes too comfortable, she is likely to become lazy and take her bedroom activities too much for granted. As a result, the fire she ignited in a lover often burns out. And without the necessary fuel of his admiration, her own sexual desires slowly fade away.

To keep herself at her best, she needs change—but because of her basically indolent nature, change is difficult. The result is often a stalemate in which she simply stays put.

She can be faithful to those who love her, but if their affection falters, that is her license to prowl. She can often be found in the center of a *ménage à trois*, with two men. By playing off one against the other, she rules as Queen of the roost.

She is only happy when she is the center of attention.

If people don't live up to her standards, she never puts the blame on herself. If she suffers an emotional setback, she tends to dramatize, to play the tragic heroine. It is simulated passion, not deeply felt anguish. She is striving for effect, not to express genuine emotion. The truth is that whatever tragedy comes her way is usually self-created.

She believes she is too idealistic, and that is why she's destined for disappointment. The truth is that she tends to love the "wrong" person, or to turn off "Mr. Right" by her unwise and overly demanding lovemaking.

She has a great talent for creating her own unhappiness.

In money matters she tends to be careless. She likes to spend money—and mainly on herself. A creature who adores luxury, she therefore favors a mate who has the wherewithal to keep her purringly content. Self-indulgence is a marked characteristic. She is a steady patron of hairdressers, buys clothing that is striking and dramatic, adores jewelry and furs. One of her favorite hobbies is to decorate and redecorate her home, with liberal use of the color red. She gives expensive gifts and throws extravagant parties. A great hostess, she will spend lavishly to entertain but will often fail to allow for that unexpected guest. How dare anyone presume to be welcome unless *she* has personally invited him?

Other women are envious of her because in a room full of attractive men she will be the cynosure of masculine attention. She draws men toward her effortlessly, perhaps because she assumes it is right and proper that they should do her homage. If she smiles at a man it can be deceptive, however, for it does not always mean she is favorably impressed. She has a persistent, incurable need for admiration, and will employ a flirtatious manner with anyone to insure that she gets it.

Her escort of the evening, however, must never for a moment let her remain in doubt as to whether *she* is the sun in *his* heaven. That would be absolutely intolerable. Unfair? Of course. But that's the way it is. Any man who wants her is going to have to learn to live with this little idiosyncrasy.

She has a fine sense of humor, and the best way to get a point across to her is to put it in a way that will make her laugh. Her laughter tends to be loud, even raucous (a lioness's roar?). When she decides to play the clown herself, she can do it delightfully, for she has a real flair for broad slapstick.

When her sign is well aspected, she can be strongly creative. In intellectual matters she is daring, resourceful, and adventurous. In a career she does well, although sometimes she is difficult to work with because of her insistence that others perform according to her expectations. She has talent but too often has little to show for it.

Anything routine bores her. She will go a long way out of her way to avoid the humdrum. Distance lends enchantment. She yearns toward the romantic places on travel posters: the Spanish Steps, the Acropolis, the Taj Mahal—each calls with its special siren song.

In any of her endeavors, she rejects criticism. And

she strongly resists self-criticism also. As one Leo woman friend told me, "Why should I run myself down—when I'm the person with whom I have to spend the rest of my life?"

An exasperated male, trampled underfoot by a domineering Leo mistress, once complained: "When the meek finally inherit the earth, where will all the Leos go?"

HER SEX LIFE

Don't expect her to meet you halfway. Because she is so convinced that any man is lucky to possess her, she sees no reason to have to lure him on.

Leo likes to carry on what she considers innocent flirtations, expressions of a free-floating libido. She will not pant after any man, for she is too self-content and self-satisfied to be sexually aggressive. Her aim is simply to make herself admired.

Her attitude is best described as sleek, lascivious, enticing—and lazy. It seems as if she is aware, by instinct, of how strongly men react to her. A crook of her imperious finger, and they hasten to obey her regal command. It *is* a command, not an invitation, for she cannot imagine any man who would dare to refuse it.

When a lover disappoints her, she does not rebuke or harangue him. Her silent contempt is a far more deadly weapon. Words are not required to express sovereign disapproval. Many a man has been withered by Leo's disdain, and very few ever have the courage for a repeat performance. They gather their rent and tattered shreds of ego and creep painfully away.

She is rarely moody, even when in love. Her basic disposition is optimistic, cheerful, and introspection is not for her. She does not torment herself about her desires. Why should she? Whatever Leo wants, Leo gets.

If a man makes himself important in her life, he can expect to be treated royally—as befits a royal consort. She creates an atmosphere of splendor and beauty in her home, where she will entertain lavishly. Although she will dress in very provocative fashions, what she is doing is not trying to seduce but to manipulate her lover—and there is a significant difference. When the moment comes for her to preen her charms, there will be a slow, voluptuous unveiling—not so much for his pleasure as for her pleasure in watching his dazzled admiration. Woe betide the lover who misunderstands this and tries to take her too quickly or by force. That's when the lioness shows her claws!

She doesn't feel any particular need to be original or creative in her boudoir behavior. Like the male of her sign, her instinct is for the conventional and straightforward. It all seems perfectly clear and simple and right to her. Why gild the lily?

When her passions are aroused, though, she will become a fiercely responsive sex partner, and there are plenty of bedmates around who have the scars to prove it. Then she expects to be praised for her sexual prowess. She knows she is a healthy, lusty animal—the queen of the jungle cats.

In the sex act, she tries to dominate but will usually settle for an equal partnership. In foreplay, she enjoys having her face and ears and neck gently laved by her lover's tongue. She also likes him to run his tongue up from her legs to her inner thighs. Her favorite method of having sex is to allow the man to penetrate halfway, then to alternate thrusts with him in a cooperating maneuver. She likes to make love with the lights on so her partner can admire her body and comment on it. Her almost compulsive need to show off leads her to prefer the woman-above position, where the man can continue to look up and admire the statuesque beauty of her body. In this woman-above position, she gets satisfaction by leaning forward and allowing a lover to take as much of her breast as possible into his mouth.

A lover's admiration is an essential part of sex for her. She always chooses her bras and panties carefully, making sure she will be her most provocative when she undresses for him. Leo women often wear wispy cut-out bras that make their nipples available for manipulation, or wear cut-out panties that make their front and rear available. On occasion, she will wear nothing but garter belt and stockings. One Leo woman I know has Polaroid pictures taken of herself during the sex act with various lovers and puts them in a scrapbook.

Leo's calm and positive approach to sex is reassuring to men worried about their virility. She's so sure everything is going to work out fine that it usually does.

And why shouldn't it? The lucky devil is making love to *her!*

Warning: Her instinct to dominate occasionally takes extreme forms.

Because Leo resents having to live in a man's world, she often assumes his role in the sex act. She's the kind who will wear a dildo and force him to bend over before her so she can penetrate him anally. She may even insist that he kiss and lick her shoes, her gloved hands, or her leatherbound breasts.

Leo enjoys the flicking of a tongue in her vagina and wants the tempo and pressure to increase until she reaches orgasm. While some oralists prefer to alternate tongue with finger manipulation, the woman born under this sign wants the tongue only and expects the man to swallow her love juice. She considers this kind of oral-genital sex as paying homage to the "Queen."

One Leo woman told me she persuaded her lover

to have the restraining membrane under his tongue cut in order to permit deeper penetration of her vagina!

I have heard of instances in which a Leo woman insisted that her lover wear rubber diapers so that she could assume the dominant role and discipline him. One particularly accommodating lover, I'm informed, would actually wet his diapers and then wait for her to change him.

Her leonine need to rule also attracts her to very young boys, for they are more inclined to offer the blind, unquestioning adoration that she desires. In return, she will teach them about sex and make them virtual prisoners of love.

THE MALE

This fellow expects to be noticed wherever he goes. He is very attractive to women and knows it. When he walks into a room women are aware of him, and other men look at him with envy.

He admires beautiful women but does not like them to talk loudly or dress garishly. As his consort, she must always behave properly. He is the one who must get all the attention!

He likes the outdoors, particularly in the daytime when the Sun, his ruler, is visible. And he enjoys competitive sports—at which he excels. You might think he would fear the inevitable defeat that comes to everyone in such fierce competition. But Leo knows too well how to turn defeat into victory. This is his moment on stage and he will prove himself masterful, kingly in his conduct toward the lucky victor. Indeed, he will prove so magnanimous that it will probably confuse most onlookers into thinking he actually won! Certainly they will believe, as he does, that only some perverse accident of fate denied him the triumph to which his superior skills entitled him.

Leo is definitely an extrovert—expansive, generous, outgoing. He loves to laugh. He is not a big-mouth or a phony, but occasionally he can be a bully. He revels in luxury and thinks the best of everything is none too good for him. That usually works out well, for if it belongs to him he thinks it is the very best. He will brook no argument about that.

Halfway measures are not for him. When he goes into a fight, it is likely to become a grand and glorious battle. When there's romance, it has to shoot sparks—or more likely become a bonfire!

He will gamble with life, with love, and with money. He never considers it reckless to go against the odds, for he feels it is his destiny to win.

Men like him because, while he plays the big shot, he is always willing to pick up the check. Women like him because he is masterful, fiery, intense.

He is demonstrative, open-handed, and a valuable friend. If need arises, he will take great risks, endure great dangers to guard the safety of those dear to him.

Invariably genial, he is usually quite popular. Even those who find his ego hard to live with at close quarters have nothing personal against him. They like him—from a safe distance.

Initially you may find his overweening assurance a bit offputting. But if you are perceptive, you will understand that he is curiously vulnerable. He needs other people to share his own high opinion of himself—and will go to almost any lengths to win them over.

You can never go wrong by flattering him, for nothing you say is likely to surpass his high opinion of himself. This is his Achilles heel, for a silver tongue can influence his decisions. He is easily wheedled—into a loan, a raise, a favor, or even marriage.

He is always falling in or out of love. Romance is not a word to him, it is a way of life. He is only happy when regally wining and dining with a lovely adoring feminine creature. And sooner or later he will find one whose admiration he cannot do without—and marry her. There are not many bachelors under this sign and, alas, their judgment about women is not always the best. Although he expresses a royal contempt for women of loose virtue, he is easily victimized by exactly this type. They know how to play on his central weakness—his vanity.

His work is often careless, but he is very good at covering up. Sometimes he will disguise a hasty and impulsive job with the frills and decorative touches at which he excels. If he can't, he will excuse himself by saying he has no patience with details or that such chores belong to lesser people. Somehow he'll manage to get across the idea that others have failed him. After a while, this can exasperate his coworkers, but Leo doesn't worry too much about the feelings of others.

Although he can be creative in business, it is usually not in a deep or meaningful way. He is a showman, a producer, who seeks always for the flashy superficial effect. That is enough to satisfy him.

He becomes angry when he doesn't get his own way, and he doesn't even like to hear contrary opinions. That last-ditch Congressional defender of Richard Nixon who proclaimed, "My mind is closed on this matter—don't confuse me with the facts," was expressing a belligerence that is typical of Leo.

If all does not go well, he tends to sulk. You have to be very careful not to provoke him at such times. However, he doesn't languish long in a depression. There are too many challenges out there waiting to be met and conquered by the King of the jungle.

Leo is jealous. Although he dwells on the mountaintop, he is afraid of being dragged down into the valley of competition with lesser mortals.

If you have a lover or husband born under this

sign, beware—but beware!—of making him jealous. He can react physically. He is the kind who will beat up a man who flirts with his woman—then beats her up when he gets her home.

HIS SEX LIFE

He needs women as much as he needs food and water.

He approaches each new encounter as if it were a glorious drama—an experience not to be filed under forget, an opportunity to exhibit his prowess. Each time he dates a woman he expects it to be a glorious, unforgettable experience.

He has a strongly sexual personality. His domineering personality simply brushes aside rules and conventions.

A woman who goes with a Leo male should be guided by one very important rule: never, never tease. What you promise you had better deliver. Leo doesn't like to play games. If you are not prepared to follow through, stay home and practice your knitting. He believes a woman should always be willing and able because he's always ready.

On the other hand, his immense self-confidence can be beguiled by a hint of mystery or aloofness. He thinks most women so anxious to gain his favor that they can hardly contain themselves. So the one who can make him feel he must pursue her is the most likely to succeed.

As a lover, he subscribes to the axiom that "action dissolves anxiety." Not for him self-doubt, timorousness, or the cautious approach. There will be no fumbling. You'll be swept off your feet into bed, taken in one great all-devouring masculine lunge.

Sometimes that defeats his own purpose. His partner gets the idea that he's out to win the sexual olympics and begins to doubt if she can make the team. It doesn't help matters that he spends so little time on foreplay. Leo is interested in nothing but his own sexual needs. Afterward, he expects a woman to congratulate him on his technique. For him, this is the pleasant "afterglow" of any sexual encounter.

His endurance is remarkable, and he has a great appetite for making love. This doesn't, as a rule, mean that he likes it more than once a day—after all, when the King has acted, who needs an encore? He may only go around once, but he does it with gusto.

Your responses must accelerate to meet his imperious demands. Don't be reticent and demure. You can start that way if you want to pique his fancy, but when Leo performs he likes a woman to show how much she is enjoying it. When she is moaning out of control or screaming and gasping with delight, she is telling him that he is master of all he surveys.

Don't ever deny Leo, for he will simply move to new hunting grounds. When not tied down by bonds of affection, he treats all women with a sovereign impartiality. As far as he's concerned, they are all open bottles that need corking.

He likes his women submissive. The standard man-above/woman-beneath posture does quite well. He knows his potency and sees no reason to embellish it with variations or divert it into other channels.

He is turned on by a woman in a "helpless" position. A favorite is to have the woman kneeling beside a bed, supporting her upper body on it. He kneels behind her, enters her, and then grasping her hips slowly stands up. This way she uses only her vaginal muscles while he controls the other movements—including the turning and rolling of her hips.

Oral sex is only acceptable if *he* is on the receiving end. For him, fellatio combines not only sexual pleasure but an attitude of adoration that preens his masculine vanity. Cunnilingus, however, is definitely *not* in his line.

Neither are the kinkier variations. He prefers the conventional forms of sexual intercourse. The missionary position is fine, and for variation he will simply turn around on the bed and plant his feet on the headboard to propel himself with more vigor.

His natural ability as a lover can flow into the wrong channels if a woman fails to play up to his enormous ego. He then turns to more offbeat kinds of self-glorification.

A favorite method is to dress up his genitals. The girl friend of a Leo once told me that he liked to wear French ticklers that looked like a squid with long rubber arms, or soft plastic rings that had oddly shaped extensions like spider legs. On one occasion he used a device that resembled a dragon's head with its tongue protruding. Knowing what brought on these adornments, I advised her to flatter him and play up to him more in the bedroom. When she did, his interest in the art of genital decoration disappeared. Like any Leo, he only wanted to be kingly and admired.

He takes great pride in the size of his sex organ and may even use electric masturbating equipment to enlarge the penis and impress his partner before intercourse. If he doesn't have a partner at hand, he will take to the streets wearing only an overcoat or a raincoat. When an attractive girl comes toward him, he will suddenly whip open the coat to reveal his penis—decorated in a way that calls full attention to the size of his phallic equipment. This sort of exhibitionism is common among Leo males.

If he has to go too long without the sexual admiration so necessary to him, Leo becomes preoccupied with the problem. He can't think of anything else. He will ignore friends, family, and business, and will finally seek relief at the more sophisticated bordellos where the girls know how to cater to his obsession.

FIRST MOVES

Their first entrance into a room is meant to make everyone else seem dim shadowy figures. So be properly impressed. Leo needs to be in the spotlight, recognized as unique and superior. Give them every possible chance to shine. Let them know that you have never met anyone like them.

Flattery is a must, and lots of it. Leo has an insatiable appetite for applause.

Don't ever crowd Leo off center stage. Always allow room for them to display their regal splendor. It helps if you are dependent or can suggest subtly that your happiness, even your life, is subject to their royal whim.

Overdoing it? With anyone else, perhaps. Never with Leo. Leo accepts this as confirmation of a simple fact.

If this sort of behavior makes you feel foolish, then refine it to where you can live with it. But never withhold appreciation or flattery. Leo can't live without it.

If you have an argument in which you know you're right and can't give in, there is a court of last resort. Appeal to Leo's sense of humor. They really love to laugh, although the laugh can never be on them.

Leo appreciates the arts, theater, and literature, and also likes to be where the excitement is, so don't pass up the opening of an art gallery, a movie or play premiere, or a fashionable literary cocktail party. The best way to get a ticket is through a charitable organization sponsoring such events. For a contribution (not as much as you'd think) you get a prized ducat. The contribution is tax deductible, and your Leo will be impressed.

On dates, don't count pennies. If you're courting a Leo woman, don't even look in your wallet. She admires extravagance and agrees that the best is hardly good enough for her. Don't show up at her door with a beat-up Volkswagen. She prefers flashy cars. In fact, she has a weakness for luxury, for ostentatious display, and a deep-down unspoken conviction that she belongs in High Society. If you're thinking of giving a gift, make it splashy. Give her something in which to make a dramatic entrance. A fox boa or a long, sweeping red velvet cape. Her favorite jewel is the ruby.

If you're wooing a Leo man, give perfectly appointed dinners in which he is treated as the guest of honor—the stellar attraction of the evening. You can't afford it? Then take him to visit friends where he will be appreciated and praised. Steer the conversation around to him and his achievements. That's all Leo really wants, and it doesn't have to cost a lot.

When the Big Moment arrives, let it be in their bedroom. It will be fit for a King or a Queen. If that can't be arranged, try to make sure it's the best room at the best hotel. (The more posh the better.) Remember that Leo needs the right setting to perform, so provide it. Don't be penny wise and love foolish.

EROGENOUS ZONES

All right, let's assume that you've got Leo in the properly regal surroundings. Where shall the action begin?

You might begin in the bath. Try rubbing Leo with a loofah sponge until the skin turns rosy. The back is a particularly vulnerable area. Work gently down along the spine to the base, then on the way up linger a little in the small of the back. Leo will be purring—and probably inviting you into the tub!

With male Leo, try raking your fingernails lightly over his back during lovemaking. You'll excite him to greater effort and more masterful performance.

Turn on a female Leo by running the fringes of a shawl (cashmere is best) from the shoulder to the small of her back. Follow this treatment with a soft bristle brush, the kind barbers use to apply talcum powder. Go over the same area, lingering a little longer in that sensitive small of the back. By then, she'll be a passionate lioness.

Useful hint: During preliminaries with a Leo woman, look for a sign of sexual arousal in a skin flush that begins at the stomach area and slowly spreads to her breasts, throat, and neck. The intensity of the flush will be in direct proportion to the amount of stimulation. When she's the right shade, she's yours!

LAST MOVES

How to break off the affair? No problem. If you've read carefully until now, you probably know how. But here's a refresher:

Talk about yourself. Monopolize the conversation.

Contradict them.

When they start talking about their problems or delivering their opinions, yawn.

Forget their birthday, Valentine's Day, the anniversary of the day you met, or the first time you went to bed together. Send a card with a jovial "Better Late Than Never!"

Don't bother to tell them they're wonderful.

Criticize how they dress, what kind of friends they have, how their home or apartment is decorated.

Always let him or her know that your career, your social life, and your sexual satisfaction come first.

Never dress properly. Lounge around in your oldest, dirtiest, shabbiest. And *don't* change when you go out.

If you attend a movie, make it the local third-run

and choose the sleaziest sex film. Exclaim over the glamor and excitement of the lovemaking in the film, implying that Leo could learn a good deal from it.

Attack their sexual prowess. Imply that it's all been actually pretty routine.

Deliberately excite their jealousy.

Be thrifty.

Puncture their vanity with ridicule.

Leo will soon be gone, to play King or Queen in some other part of the jungle.

YOUR SENSUAL GUIDE

LEO and ARIES: This couple is drawn together, for they share a powerful interest in sex. Both have kindling, passionate natures. Aries's compulsion to lead comes up against Leo's desire to rule, and that's like the conflict between the irresistible force and the immovable object. However, their physical rapport is great and should overwhelm problems. A joyful affair, a fine marriage.

LEO and TAURUS: Their romantic duet can turn into a vocal tug-of-war. Both are too set on having their own way, and the contest of wills can become explosive. They can have an affectionate sexual relationship, but Leo's exuberance will prove annoying to quiet, sedate Taurus. Extravagant Leo will be constantly irked by Taurus closely watching the buck. A possible affair, but a longer liaison is doubtful.

LEO and GEMINI: Gemini has to be clever to keep Leo in thrall, for while Leo is easygoing and tolerant, cuckoldry does not suit its royal image. Gemini's natural instinct to find ways to get along should see them through. Leo is stimulated, fascinated and sometimes exasperated by Gemini. Since Leo is the stronger personality, it will dominate without effort. A fun affair, a fine marriage.

LEO and CANCER: Leo is looking for a more casual affair than Cancer, who wants to become involved. Cancer wants more than just sexual passion; it wants the stamina, the durability, and the little attentions that go with love. Leo may be disposed to give that if it gets all of Cancer's love in return with a little worship thrown in. If not, bad vibes. If so, the stars in their courses look down and approve.

LEO and LEO: In the bedroom, as elsewhere, Leo tends to think in terms of first-person singular. The big question is: Can two "I's" make a "We"? Well, kings and queens usually refer to themselves as "we"—so why not? Both are very romantic and sexually compatible. Each has to let the other shine and to share the spotlight if necessary. That isn't always possible, of course, but when it is: Long Live the King! Long Live the Queen!

LEO and VIRGO: Leo is more sexually responsive than Virgo, and that can spell trouble in the bedroom. Leo's royal extravagance also causes conservative, prudent Virgo a royal pain somewhere in the anatomy. Virgo doesn't want to be dominated, Leo doesn't want to do anything else. If Virgo starts to criticize, Leo will start to roar. They might have a brief clandestine affair. Marriage? Ha!

LEO and LIBRA: Leo's approach to sex is more physical and direct than Libra's. However, both will have an entertaining time, for Libra can also be quite passionate with the right inducement. Easygoing Libra must never neglect to pay proper homage to Leo's boudoir mastery and must restrain a proclivity toward too much candor. Leo has to guard its temper. Otherwise, a very good match and probably an enduring one.

LEO and SCORPIO: Roman candles, dazzlers, and sparklers in the bedroom. This can do a lot to offset other troubles. Scorpio's jealous anger offends Leo. Scorpio won't offer the respect and admiration that Leo needs. Scorpio will try to be possessive, which Leo cannot abide, and each wants to dominate. An affair can be exciting. A marriage should be avoided.

LEO and SAGITTARIUS: Both signs have a keen sense of love as adventure. They are extroverted, passionate, and pursue their own sexual inclinations without awakening resentment in the other. Both desire frequent intercourse. Sagittarius stimulates and inspires Leo, and Leo evokes from Sagittarius whatever loyalty this sign is capable of. An affair is great fun, and a happy marriage is guaranteed.

LEO and CAPRICORN: Capricorn's practical approach puts a halter on Leo's expansive, optimistic personality. There are fundamental differences between them. Leo's glamor will be dimmed and even diminished in this relationship. Capricorn is not as romantic or affectionate as Leo and can be too demanding. Leo's extravagance will be annoying to Capricorn. A shack-up can be pleasant, a marriage probably not.

LEO and AQUARIUS: Aquarius sparks Leo's sexual individuality and lends excitement to their lovemaking. While Leo is intrigued, it is also angered by Aquarius's tendency to analyze and expose. That shakes Leo's confidence in its sovereign powers. Also, the emphasis on unorthodoxy in the bedroom will get on Leo's nerves. Transient sex partners, impossible marital partners.

LEO and PISCES: Demonstrative, ebullient Leo rubs shy, introverted Pisces the wrong way. Leo isn't that anxious to probe the mystery of Pisces's bedroom behavior. Both are more prone to receive than to give. An initial magnetic attraction builds toward an eventual explosion. Pisces is the weaker sign, and its lack of ambition disturbs Leo. When Pisces sulks, Leo's pride prohibits showing sympathy. A difficult affair, a most unhappy marriage.

VIRGO

August 23–September 22

THE FEMALE

More Virgo women are spinsters than are any other sign in the zodiac. The trouble is, she can't find a man who lives up to her standards.

She tends to make superficial judgments of people, i.e., whether they are neat and hygenically clean. As a result, she can miss out on meeting compatible persons of either sex.

The key to understanding her is to think of her not as cerebral or cold, but as someone very much in control. Her emotions are the same as those of other women, but she keeps them under a tighter rein. Her secret longings are likely to remain secret.

She tends to be rather serious and dignified. Modesty is a natural endowment, and you won't find her boasting about her achievements. She has excellent manners and always conducts herself like a lady—except when provoked. She believes a lady is someone who never offends—except deliberately. Then watch out. In fact, you'd better take cover. For she can unleash a verbal assault that will reduce even a well-entrenched ego to a mass of whimpering Jell-o.

She believes in self-improvement and studies hard to better herself and her position in life. She is particularly interested in learning about literature, music, and art, and many Virgo women develop acute and perceptive critical powers.

She worries too much. This is partly because she is convinced that she can reason her way through to a solution to almost any problem. She trusts her intellect more than her intuition and, when confronted with a problem, she will chew on it like a dog with a meaty bone until its shape is all bare and clear to see.

She can be generous, patient, and kind—but she is also very determined, a cool pussycat whose head is always in command of her heart. When she is set on a course of action, even a direct hit by a mortar shell will not turn her aside.

Her energy is enough for two or three women, and she will tackle any task with the conviction that no one can perform it more efficiently than she. In any enterprise, she takes every possible precaution against failure. Like a trapeze artist working without a net, she wants to know there will be another trapeze waiting when she comes out of that high triple somersault through the air.

Her domain is the home. This is where she rules, and a wise man will give her sway. Her dwelling place looks as if no one has ever lived in it. She wants everything in its place and has a place for everything. A wise shopper, she knows how to stretch a dollar until it squeaks.

She knows what a man wants. If he can't see it himself, she will help him to analyze the situation. She's very good at analyzing. Her goals are practical and attainable with the right determination and drive.

If she marries, it is usually late in life. She will be a perfect housekeeper, an excellent mother (though perhaps a little stern), and an interesting companion to her husband. Sex is a matter of procreation rather than pleasure, and this can be frustrating, for she is usually pretty and keeps her goods looks well into middle age.

Socially, she likes small parties, immaculately catered. Sloppy eaters, careless smokers, too-casual dressers will not be invited more than once. She excels at intellectual parlor games.

If she has to work for a living, her exacting habits are carried over into the business world. She is very good with figures and can be a very good certified public accountant. She can also be a perfect private secretary, particularly if the business is one that features self-improvement. In any job, she demands a salary that insures her independence. In a really hard choice, however, she will put up with being underpaid if she is treated fairly and with kindness and consideration.

Usually quite objective and unemotional, her judgment may be clouded in one area—where her lover is concerned. She can't see his faults and weaknesses. She is loyal to her idealized image of him and her feelings run deep, though she may not be openly demonstrative or affectionate.

She tends to treat a man as if he were some kind of virgin territory, ready to be explored, surveyed, developed, and improved. She knows her way around a man's psyche—for she has an almost psychic knowledge of motivations—and will usually end up as mistress of all she surveys.

She expects everyone to be as neat and clean as she is. Not for her the squalid charms of the celebrated Dr. Samuel Johnson, who once sat near an elegant and perfumed lady at the dinner table. "Dr. Johnson, you smell," she remarked. Dr. Johnson, who wrote the first English dictionary and had a rare sense for the precise word, replied: "No, Madam, *you* smell. *I* stink."

If the lady was a Virgo, she was not amused.

But if she was a Virgo, you can bet she *was* a lady.

HER SEX LIFE

She has no illusions about sex and wishes everyone would not magnify its importance. She simply can't believe that thunder rolls or lightning strikes when two bodies join in what is, after all, a perfectly natural function.

She doesn't like men who come on like a Concorde jet trying to make a landing. She prefers men who have enough self-discipline to wait for a relationship to develop to where sex is inevitable. She doesn't think of it in those terms, of course. More likely she would say that romance is important also, and that anyone who emphasizes the purely physical aspects doesn't understand or appreciate the real meaning of making love. She sees courtship not as a preliminary to be gotten through as quickly as possible so mattress thumping can begin, but as the gracious, lovely overture to a symphonic climax. She enjoys going to bed, but she isn't going to go into sentimental rhapsodies about it.

Given a chance, she would rather fill her bedroom with the scent of fresh flowers than a musky, provocative perfume. And she won't make a dramatic appearance wearing nothing but Indian love beads on her naked body. This isn't a scene from a movie, dear boy, it's real life. Both of you know what you're there for.

Once she decides to give herself, you won't be disappointed. Her feminine grace and modesty, her gently yielding warmth, turn on those who are tired of simulated fireworks. Everything will work out to your entire satisfaction.

The terms of surrender will probably be discussed in advance, covering such details as where it is going to take place. She prefers her own home because she is more in control of things there. Bring champagne.

Don't be surprised if she suggests a shower or a bath for two before the main action. That gives more time for the all-important preliminaries and pleases her compulsive need for cleanliness. She may give you a good scrubbing with a brush before allowing any other contact. Don't be offended. It's just Virgo's way, so relax and enjoy it.

The bedroom will be dimly lit or with no lights. The bed will be freshly made, the room itself immaculate, and good music may be playing on the stereo. The telephone will be disconnected. Virgo foresees everything.

Do with her what you will. That is, provided you stop short of what she considers abnormal, grotesque, or animalistic. If that seems to rule out a lot, you may be right. But she sets the boundaries of what will delight her.

Within those boundaries, she more than makes up for any feeling you have of being fenced in. She can turn a kiss into an erotic experience almost equal to intercourse. To please a lover, she may go as far as nibbling, sucking, licking, and other forms of oral gratification. And she'll become an artist at it. Her highest sexual pleasure is derived from making you happy. But in the arithmetic of lustful behavior, the highest number she'll get to is sixty-nine.

After foreplay, unless you indicate otherwise, she will immediately assume the missionary position. But don't worry. If you have something else in mind, she'll go along. Just explain beforehand what you want, and then depend on her to do her utmost to please. After all, sex is a household chore to her, like making and serving coffee in the morning. Like the women in the TV coffee commercials, she won't be content unless she gets it right.

However, if you want to touch her magic button and set her own sexual juices flowing, try mutual masturbation—particularly in the position where she spreads her legs over your face and lets you tongue her, while she grasps and fondles your penis behind her back. Pure ecstasy!

She does have a few sexual hang-ups, usually involved with punishment. The reason is clear. When she does anything that conflicts with her moral scruples, she expects to be punished. Using a paddle on her buttocks is a physical rebuke that she understands. But it also has an erotic excitement for her, and such espisodes usually end in sexual intercourse with whoever is paddling her. Failing that, she will sometimes masturbate herself afterward with the handle of the paddle!

If she feels she enjoys sex too much, she may even make her punishment an integral part of the act. One Virgo woman made her lover strap an extra-large dildo to his waist and enter her anus, causing enough pain to counteract the pleasure he was giving her.

Some women born under this sign are unable to participate in sexual intercourse without a third party. This third person acts as a "conscience," dressing her down verbally while she copulates—thereby freeing her to satisfy her desires. A variation combines a verbal harangue with corporal punishment. A whip or paddle is vigorously applied to her backside while orders are given like, "Fellate your lover!" The one inflicting punishment must continue to do so even as Virgo complies.

All this is discussed beforehand and no one is deceived by it, but in an obscure way Virgo woman feels clean because she was "forced" to take part.

THE MALE

Ruled by Mercury, planet of the mind, he has a keen, orderly, discriminating intellect, and excels in mental work. He is interested in almost anything that will further his personal career or his fortune. One of the first things he wants to know about other people is whether they have money and how they are taking care of it. In his view, it is sinful to waste money, for it is a measure of personal accomplishment and a gauge for estimating the value of others.

No one can talk him into a venture that seems impractical. Some instinct warns him when he is skating too near thin ice, and he simply veers away. Or perhaps I'm being unfair to call it an instinct. Virgo's keenly practical, analytical mind can uncover the hidden risks in any given proposition. When he says no, he is not acting on a hunch but rendering a verdict that is based on the facts as he seems them—and no one sees them better. And you can depend on his "no" as the last word on the subject. When he says no, he doesn't mean maybe or perhaps. He means no.

He has a fine discrimination in choosing friends and lovers, and rarely makes mistakes. Certainly he never makes the same mistake twice. He subscribes to the adage, "Once burned, shame on him; twice burned, shame on me!"

Because he expects other people to live up to his standards, he is often hypercritical. That doesn't help to win friends or influence women. No one likes to have his or her character examined too minutely for flaws. Virgo can't help doing it. He also finds it difficult to flatter anyone.

Usually of a nervous temperament, he requires peaceful surroundings to function at his best. This also accounts for his devotion to fresh air, exercise, and a regular regimen. He believes in looking after his health. He also believes that if you want to get ahead in the world, you must use your leisure time to sharpen your abilities.

He finds women a curiosity, something to be examined, experimented with, coddled, and catered to. As for sex, it is just one of many facets of life, an experience that one should not overlook—provided one has the time and the inclination.

Most bachelors are born under this sign. Virgo men are too busy being perfectionists at their work to bother with romance. They are systematic and careful, and have a strong sense of responsibility and duty. In the pecking order of a large corporation, you will often find Virgo second in command. He is methodical and reliable, but his modesty never gets him full credit for a job well done.

He is dependable, smart, a hard, conscientious worker. Give him a problem, and he'll usually come up with a solution. If he takes a while, that's because he is diligently doing research and gathering information from every available source. He does his homework. If there's one thing he hates, it's to be caught unprepared.

He doesn't wear trendy clothing, and you'll never find him with a scraggly beard. He is as meticulous about his personal appearance as he is about his grammar.

He isn't the most exciting date a woman ever had, but he will make her feel comfortable and happy. He won't run the gamut of passion from alpha to omega, but he also doesn't demand constant attention, won't hog the spotlight, and will always be gentle and considerate. Even when provoked, he rarely losses his temper.

When you close the door after a date, his foot won't be in the way. He'll wait to be invited into your boudoir. He's not a woman chaser; he prefers women to chase him. As a sexual partner, he's a good bet for the long haul. Other men burn themselves out in the hectic white hot flush of early passions, but Virgo is still there, rolling along like Ol' Man River, after more ardent suitors have come to shipwreck.

In his relations with a woman, he may adopt a fatherly attitude and exert a protective interest over her life. He can become an invaluable friend and counselor. If she wants more romance, she had better dig in for a long struggle. When he finally shacks up with a woman or proposes marriage, it will only be after a prolonged courtship. And it will likely be a careful decision made only after weighing whether a mate will aid his career, whether she has money enough to enhance his way of life, or whether she will make a comfortable home for him so he can pursue his activities without distraction.

In turn, he will offer a mate security, reliability, faithfulness. She can forget partying or social excitement because that is not his bag. He'd rather spend his time in the garden or reading a book. She won't have to worry about him being out at night drinking with the boys until early morning hours. No social lion, he.

She will be financially secure, but that doesn't mean she'll get everything she wants. He has a tight fist with a buck, although he prefers to call it "understanding the value of money" or "spending a dollar to get a dollar's worth." For him, the dollar paid was a dollar earned. On the other hand, he doesn't travel third class. What he really expects is full value for what he spends.

He is devoted. Don't worry about his cheating in the game of love. He plays his cards exactly as they are dealt to him. Fidelity is not just a word to him. But, as with many people who profess to have high morals, his morality can often be traced to a simple absence of desire.

Romantic excitment? No.

Security? Yes.

HIS SEX LIFE

Virgo does not go around picking up girls.

If she thinks back on how it all began, she will realize that she first suggested having dinner some evening. He is too shy to make an overture. Chances are, she only met him because they were introduced by a mutual friend or got to know each other at the office.

She had better be on time for that first date—and

for others thereafter—because punctuality is important. Other qualities he particularly admires are tactfulness, poise, good manners (including good table manners), and an ability to talk on a wide variety of topics. He prefers to choose the place to go to on a date, and he will have very definite ideas about the people he likes to visit.

You won't have to worry about him feeling your knee under the table, hugging you in public, or hanging in the doorway hoping to be invited in for "one last drink." That isn't the way he operates.

When the moment does arrive for that intimate candlelit dinner at your place (which you hope will include breakfast for two the next morning), you had better make all the arrangements with him in advance. He'll want to bring his pajamas, shaving equipment and toothbrush, a fresh shirt and tie, clean socks, and probably his alarm clock so he can get to work on time! He may even want to discuss how you like your sex before you get started.

There will be no vulgar displays of passion, no unasked-for importunity. His foreplay will be quite studied, even methodical. He has a good knowledge of female anatomy. Having boned up beforehand on exactly what turns a woman on, he will trigger the right erotic responses. His technique is esthetic rather than sensual, and the wrong vibrations affect his performance adversely. When that happens, he will blame circumstances rather than himself for the failure.

However, he is always open to suggestion, and an aggressive woman can get him to do almost anything she desires. Don't expect him to be too imaginative about sex. He will work very hard though, and a woman who does not attain orgasm has only herself to blame. Self-sacrificing Virgo will literally bend over backward to please his bedmate. Some women like it that way.

An unusual circumstance will sometimes light his fire. A Virgo man I know told me he was traveling in a bus at night with the lights out when he was propositioned by the woman sitting beside him. Since she wore no panties beneath her mini-skirt, there was no difficulty in accommodating her. Having sex with a strange woman in a bus while the other passengers were asleep or dozing was the most marvelous experience of his life. It gave him a new, wholly un-Virgolike attitude about how and where and when lovemaking should take place!

However, you can't always travel by bus. Unless stimulated, Virgo male is likely to settle for the most conventional method: the missionary position in bed at night—under the covers. But there is a variation that does appeal to him. This is where the woman rests her head on the floor, lying face down and supporting herself on her elbows, while he raises her legs into the wheelbarrow position and enters her from behind.

He responds to new techniques if they aren't introduced too forcefully. Think of him as a bud that has to be treated with loving care to bring it to the full bloom of sensual beauty.

One good tip: Bite a Virgo man softly on his buttock. That raises his temperature quicker than a hot bath. He usually gets a quick erection.

Not all the stories about Virgo male's boudoir frigidity are untrue. His de-emphasis of sex can cross over into indifference. Sometimes he will be married for years yet abstain from marital relations until the lack of use causes his penis to atrophy, making it useless as a sexual tool.

More negatively aspected, he will become voyeuristic. An innocent peek into a woman's cleavage, a fascination with tight pants that accent the vulva, an avid spectator's role at pool or beach where the women turn out in their skimpiest bikinis—all these are early signs of a tendency that can develop into an obsession with pornography. Often he will masturbate while reading sexy books or watching stag films.

He can be a strange sexual animal. One Virgo male of my acquaintance told me that he was particularly turned on by having a naked girl parade in front of him and do exercises with a cane or a broomstick. He would make her begin by holding the cane over her head and then, while keeping her legs stiff, bring it down horizontally to her toes. He liked to watch this performance from the rear for the best peekaboo view of her vulva and rectum. When she began doing kneebends, holding the cane ferrule-up just in front of her, he would masturbate.

Another man born under this sign came to me for a consultation because he wanted to know what was inclining him toward his sexual hang-up. He told me that his wife was promiscuous, but he actually encouraged her to be because he liked to watch her having sex with other men. He hid in a closet with a peep-hole in the door and brought a jug or a narrow-topped thermos with him to masturbate in.

I hardly needed any confirmation from his solar chart. He was a fairly typical Virgo male in the grip of sexual obsession, and his situation was complicated by the fact that he was approaching middle age and beginning to feel that his last chance for a normal sex life had passed him by. It was a case of not in our stars, Dear Brutus, but in our calendar.

FIRST MOVES

They are attracted to anyone with charm, grace, and poise.

They admire wit and talent. If you have neither, then save up *bon mots* from columns, from books about such celebrated wits as George S. Kaufman, Dorothy Parker, Robert Benchley. As a substitute for talent, try good taste: Show him or her that you too appreciate the arts, music, and theater. If you want to really make an impression, bone up on the critical reviews first, so you can discourse with authority.

Virgo enjoys clever repartee—but it should be spontaneous, not rehearsed. Virgo thinks Johnny Carson is much funnier when ad-libbing than during that opening ten-minute monolog.

They are devoted to their work, true work-aholics. You will find him or her among the hardy few staying late at the office to clear off their desks. Or at a party they will be helping to clear the dishes, empty the ashtrays, and wipe off wetmarks—while the party is in full swing.

The best approach? Find a topic that's a cut above the ordinary. Forget that ribald story that made such a good introduction for you elsewhere. It isn't appreciated here. Above all, don't try the swinging approach: "Will you or won't you; should we or shouldn't we?"

Don't take Virgo to a flashy or expensive place. Avoid the race track or any clip joint where money seems to be thrown away. Virgo hates waste. If you're thinking of a gift, nothing is better than a good book or a good music album. Their taste in clothes is classic and understated—discreet silk shirts or scarves. In perfume, she likes the smell of flowers or lemon.

Remember: Virgo wants to respect you, to believe that your education, cultural interests, and/or social standing are equal or superior to theirs.

Offbeat suggestion: Try taking male Virgo to a business trade show where the latest business equipment is on display. He's always interested in ways to improve efficiency. Or take her to where she can see the latest in kitchen equipment and labor-saving home devices—perhaps a big warehouse or department store sale. One clever fellow, unable to make a date with a pretty young Virgo, in desperation threw a Tupperware party at his home to which he invited friends and the young lady. He not only got free kitchenware—he got the girl!

EROGENOUS ZONES

When you're looking for a physical trigger to turn Virgo on and matters have progressed to the point where you can play touch and feel, don't overlook the stomach.

In Virgo, this entire area from crotch to lower chest is responsive to the tongue, the moving of fingers lightly across, simple caresses, or even feather-light touches of a lover's hair. A fingernail moving horizontally from one side to the other will evoke a tingling sensation.

Sensuous thrills may be obtained by laving the stomach area with a sponge, soap, and warm water. Virgo also particularly likes the feeling of the spray from a shower nozzle directed at this area. Don't forget this if you are enjoying a shower for two prior to a bedroom joust (which is a wonderful idea because Virgo is very turned on by cleanliness).

If the bathtub has a small seat, have your Virgo woman sit on your lap while you penetrate her from behind, allowing the shower to caress her stomach and pubic area in front.

While lying in bed, use a gentle circular massaging on your Virgo that draws in toward the belly button. Culminate this by putting the tip of your tongue directly into the belly button and continuing the same circular motion. You'll get quicker results than you bargained for!

LAST MOVES

Virgos will overlook a great deal and are generally reluctant to end a relationship. However, they do have a breaking point. If you want to put the romance into reverse gear, here's a guaranteed foolproof list of how to do it:

Use vulgar language.

Don't bathe often. Dress sloppily. Drop cigarette butts into the coffee cup. Let your living quarters really look lived in.

Never be on time for a date.

Take Virgo to a topless club or a porno movie.

Be unsympathetic.

Resent any criticism.

Be overly demonstrative in public.

Question any decision Virgo makes. Or, alternatively make decisions without consulting Virgo.

Tell dirty jokes and scatological stories in mixed company.

Gamble for money.

That loud noise you just heard was Virgo slamming the door—on the way out.

YOUR SENSUAL GUIDE

VIRGO and ARIES: Virgo may be intrigued by audacious Aries. But Aries needs a passionate bedmate and Virgo is too inhibited to fill the bill. Aries is always looking for adventure, and Virgo is inclined to stick to the tried and true. Virgo likes stimulating talk; Aries like stimulating action. An unlikely affair, and a marriage certainly not made in heaven.

* * *

VIRGO and TAURUS: Taurus likes to enjoy its sex without too much fuss and bother, while Virgo likes to analyze, examine—and perhaps criticize. Otherwise Virgo proves a willing if not passionate partner for Taurus. In other areas there is true compatibility. Both are materialistic, practical, admire efficiency, and are homebodies. A happy (though not too exciting) affair, and a decidedly workable marriage.

VIRGO and GEMINI: They may get along sexually because Virgo is rather impersonal in this area and Gemini is not usually too passionate. However, Gemini has a much more impulsive attitude toward making love and isn't likely to put up with Virgo's nagging. Gemini needs freedom and won't accept Virgo's desire to dominate and control. Virgo considers Gemini flighty and irresponsible. A possible affair, but don't sign a marriage license.

VIRGO and CANCER: Virgo provides the emotional security that Cancer needs and the little attentions that prove affection. Cancer's dependence finds its perfect answer in Virgo's needs to be protective. Cancer's imagination is stimulating to Virgo, and Cancer's anxiety to please deepens Virgo's affections. Both will come out of their shell and begin to enjoy life. An ardent affair, a lasting marriage.

VIRGO and LEO: Leo is highly sexed, and Virgo is interested more in security than in a roll in the hay. There will be squabbles about this and about Virgo's unfortunate tendency to criticize—for Leo is, and must remain, above criticism. Virgo's practical, down-to-earth approach also conflicts with Leo's expansive, optimistic nature. An affair is probably a one-night stand; a marriage can be a disaster.

* * *

VIRGO and VIRGO: They share a sexual reserve and consider a love relationship as a basis for something more important—a life partnership. Demands in the bedroom will not be excessive, but that doesn't rule out complaint and criticism about what does take place. Virgo simply can't help it. A tense affair, but marriage is well-aspected if boredom doesn't set in too early.

VIRGO and LIBRA: Loving and affectionate Libra is rebuffed by Virgo's cool and analytical manner. Virgo is overcritical and undermines Libra's self-confidence. Libra's occasional frivolity also displeases Virgo, who is intolerant of any indiscretion. The signs have little in common. An affair is difficult, and it is better not to contemplate marriage.

VIRGO and SCORPIO: These two are basically compatible, although Virgo does tend to chill Scorpio's sexual ardor. Scorpio keeps trying to make Virgo wake up to more sensual enjoyment, and Virgo wonders why Scorpio is so aggressive—can't they be friends as much as lovers? If Virgo is willing to compromise, Scorpio stays tractable. An interesting affair with good vibes for a permanent union.

VIRGO and SAGITTARIUS: Sagittarius's happy-go-lucky approach to love can drive Virgo crazy. Virgo's sense of security really suffers in this relationship. Sagittarius makes little or no attempt to understand Virgo's needs and is impatient with Virgo's prudent, prudish attitudes toward sex. Inevitably, Sagittarius starts looking for other sexual outlets. The two might make it for a weekend together, but not for life.

VIRGO and CAPRICORN: Virgo is sexually drawn toward Capricorn but the fireworks may fizzle. Virgo will find itself taking second place to Capricorn's extra-boudoir interests, and this may cause a certain conflict. Otherwise the two signs work harmoniously together. Both are very practical, emotionally reserved, thrifty, and active intellectually. An affair could be rather dull, a marriage will be strong and good.

VIRGO and AQUARIUS: Both tend to think of romance more as an intellectual pastime than a physical exercise. This ideal relationship is marred by the intrusion of other practical differences. Virgo is straitlaced about sex, and Aquarius veers toward the erratic. Virgo thinks Aquarius neglectful; Aquarius thinks Virgo unresponsive. Love will tend to diminish rather than grow with time. A realistic affair, an unwise marriage.

VIRGO and PICES: For Virgo, love is closely allied with security, physical needs with mental compatibility. For Pisces, love is all-encompassing, the central charm of life, beauty and romance and emotional excitement. Virgo's careful, disciplined approach to sex goes all awry when it comes up against the grandiose, unrestricted desires of Pisces. Unless Virgo's reserve can be broken, this makes an uncomfortable short-term liaison and an unrewarding marriage.

LIBRA

September 23–October 22

THE FEMALE

Women born under this sign are noted for their beauty and delicate complexion, and for a deep aversion to what is unattractive. She has an instinct for the finer things. She is fastidious in manner and dress, wears subtle, sensuous (and expensive) perfume, loves beautiful jewelry, and tries to surround herself with luxury. She admires beauty in all its manifestations, in music, art, architecture—and people. The place she lives in always has a touch of elegance.

This same fastidiousness applies to men. She wears an escort like a diamond on her finger, to add to her sense of self. Any man who can't do that would be well advised to stay clear of this woman.

She sees herself as if she were reflected on a screen where she can watch her movements and appreciate her graceful loveliness. However, she is not uncritical. She expects her image to measure up to high standards and will make what corrections are necessary. Small wonder that Libra women are considered the epitome of charm.

Her tendency toward fickleness cannot be denied. She tries to lure any attractive male she meets, but she will soon move on to a new conquest. She can forget quicker than a mirror. Except in unusual instances, her affections are rather shallow and don't last long.

Because Venus rules her Sun sign, the Libran woman is skilled in the arts of love.

However, don't forget that aversion to whatever she considers unattractive. If you happen to be on out-of-condition male with sagging, pendulous belly or unmuscled, flabby arms, if you have a tendency to look female around the chest area, or if your bony knees knock, then make sure the lights are out when you get out of concealing clothes—or you may find your woman developing a very sudden migraine or even fleeing to the bathroom to lock herself in.

One Libran woman came to me indignantly wanting to know why I hadn't warned her about the man she had wanted as a potential lover. I didn't know what she was talking about. Their signs were compatible, he was tall and good-looking, a successful lawyer, and she enjoyed his company. Then she told me: On their first night together she discovered he had a penis that when erect seemed to assume the shape of a boomerang, thick at the root and shaping up thin at the top, and that the delicate pink shaft she expected was actually somewhat gnarled with blood vessels and purple at the head (glans). For most women this one physical handicap might have been overlooked in view of all the other positive factors, but not for a Libran!

The Libra female tends to prefer the artistic type rather than the commercial—an actor, singer, writer, artist, or musician rather than a businessman. A rather sharp-tongued Libran expressed it this way: "As far as I'm concerned, God only made businessmen because He needed somebody to do all the dull, unimaginative work in the world!"

Actually, Libra woman is not always interested in men *per se*. Chiefly she wants to be admired. She may need a man around to keep laving her ego, but her focus is on herself. Any occasion is a setting for her, and she the jewel in its center.

She will not be hurried. There's no use telling her that the dinner invitation is for seven thirty, it is already a quarter to eight, and she is still putting on her lipstick. She won't be impressed and she will continue putting on that last finishing touch. After all, any social occasion is nothing more than an opportunity for her to be its shining star.

And perhaps she is right, for she is capable of

igniting a social evening. She enters a room like a trail of sparkling lights. Her enthusiasm inspires a similar reaction from others.

When things don't go her way, she can turn petty and carping. She expects perfection and is apt to exaggerate any faults and blemishes that keep her from having it. A particular bugaboo: an escort who even mentions money. In her opinion, money is for spending and buying, not for talking about. Talk about money bores the Libran woman. Her only interest in money is in the beautiful *things* it buys: emerald hairclips, chinchilla boas, Dom Perignon. She doesn't care about cold cash itself.

She likes reading pleasant books, seeing movies with happy endings, living in rooms filled with flowers, listening to soothing music. Even-tempered and serene, she will occasionally display an irresistible vivacity. Her euphoric moods are compensated for by "downers" in which she finds a cloud in every silver lining.

In small details she is a perfectionist. The tiniest sign of disarray will start her fussing. She's the kind who would be rearranging the deck chairs on the *Titanic* as the ship went down.

Don't try to give her orders. She won't obey them. If you persist, you will simply uncover her deep strain of stubbornness. The more pressure, the stubborner she will get. A kind word and soft persuasion are the only way to break her *won't* power.

Extremely feminine, she is also clever, articulate, hypochondriac. When her sign is afflicted she can be indecisive to a point where she sits passively waiting for guidance like a blind person who waits for a seeing-eye dog.

She's a fascinating, many-sided, conscious charmer.

HER SEX LIFE

The key word is drama. When she makes her first appearance in a nearly transparent nightgown, the light will be *behind* her for the best effect. She will have set the stage carefully for sex. Libra women enjoy watching the reactions of their lovers. And afterward she likes to know and to hear how much you've enjoyed making love to her.

She prefers a languorous approach. After all, what's the hurry? The night was made for love.

She enjoys all the preliminaries, including verbal. It's a good idea for a man to drop in a few lines of a love sonnet, if he can do it with assurance and not bumble the delivery. She understands that seduction is an art, not a physical assault. A really successful bed session is a mutual triumph. She is not a citadel to be taken by force.

Because she is sure of her sexuality, she will often try to emphasize it and be provocative in unexpected ways. She may prepare herself for the act by rubbing aromatic unguents into her skin. She may have talcumed her pubic area. One Libra woman I know has her pubic hair shaved in the shape of a small heart with her lover's initials in the center. Another wears little pendant beads which she fixes in place with adhesive so they rattle sensuously with every swaying motion of her hips while she sits astride her partner.

If you want to titillate her sense of drama, by all means try a mirrored ceiling. Or special lighting effects. She enjoys lying prone while a lover lasciviously massages her naked back, starting slightly above her buttocks and working up gently in tiny circles until reaching her shoulder blades. Then she will turn over to let her breasts be massaged the same way.

She's mistress of the Venus fly trap—women born under this sign have an usual control of the vaginal muscles. They can constrict and close to hold a male fast in her clutches. Then she can loosen them, and tighten again, at her—and his—pleasure. Some Libra women are so adept at this that they bring a man to climax without using any other muscle in their body.

If you spend the night, *don't* wake her for breakfast. She loves to sleep. Figure on a late brunch, usually with champagne, during which you can tell her all about what a wonderful bedtime you had. Afterward, you might invite her for a replay in the shower. She happens to like cleanliness too. But don't draw the shower curtain. She enjoys watching herself act and react in the wall mirror.

Good variations on the theme: Pour a few drops of champagne or brandy on her navel and sip it. If you coat your penis with honey, she'll like the taste sensation.

One warning: During oral sex, keep your hands off her hair. She is extra sensitive to any pulling on her head.

Never be animalistic. She finds it very easy to say yes when approached in the right way—and I mean yes to anything. But she will say no to the man who comes on like a boar in heat. Her body may seek sexual excess, but her mind demands moderation.

Definite no-no: Never try it in the back seat of a car at a drive-in movie. You'll waste your time and you'll probably lose the girl.

She is intensely feminine and, as noted, an instinctive exhibitionist. She's the one who wears the see-through blouse and no bra, and walks with a stride that she knows will make her breasts jounce. You can bet that the next woman who "loses" the top half of her bikini at the beach was born under the sign of Libra. And the woman sitting across from you in the bus with a mini-mini and no discernible underpanties? Strike up a conversation by asking her if she was born under the sign of the scales. You'll be right!

Libra will share her loveliness with anyone who appreciates her beauty. She dotes on her body and feels that it was made to be seen and admired. While parading nude before you (quite possibly near an open window!) she has no objection to your extravagantly praising her buttocks, the soft flowing line of abdomen to crotch, the bushiness of her pubic hair. She quite understands if you simply cannot resist the impulse to handle, fondle, and caress any of her "pretty" appendages.

Often Libra's self-admiration leads into narcissism —a condition in which she is stimulated by her own body. The difference between a masturbator and the narcissist is psychological; the latter is actually in love with her body, whereas the masturbator performs acts only for physical pleasure.

She goes in for bizarre lovemaking. In my experience as a consultant, the most genuinely imaginative variations to the sex act have been told to me (if not discovered) by Libran women. One woman stuffed a silk scarf into the anus of her male partner when he was lying on top of her, and then as he reached his climax she slowly pulled out the scarf—thereby prolonging his climax into a truly shattering orgasm! Later, she told me she had added another fillip to the method. She put several small knots into the scarf at strategic places and as she slowly drew it out, each knot stimulated her partner to further outpourings of passion. Another Libran female favored the use of a vibrator, which she touched to the male's anus at precisely the vital moment. I'm told his reactions were absolutely ecstatic! One Libran told me her lover had a great fondness for spearmint chewing gum, so she bought a pack and put all five unwrapped pieces in her vagina, protruding slightly. The next time he asked for a piece of chewing gum, she simply lifted her skirt, opened her legs, and invited him to help himself! And yet another (believe it or not, all Librans!) was the first to tell me of a way to lend an additional thrill to oral sex. She would mouth her lover's testicles and hum. This would set off a vibration that gave resonance to the act, and if he talked or hummed at the same time he sent vibrations back to her that she also found extremely stimulating!

Rely on a Libran female to figure out a way to double, or triple, the fun.

She is frequently a favorite with fetishist males, particularly for the variety of fetishism known as partialism, in which there is a fixation for a single part of the body. She is sympathetic toward anyone who happens to develop a passion for her hair, hands, toes, knees, or you name it. And why not? If she's as beautiful as she thinks she is, then all parts of her must be too!

THE MALE

He was born under the sign of the scales, so what he strives for is balance and harmony. Life may be a seesaw, first one side up, then the other, but he can't help running back and forth to try to strike an equilibrium. His sensitive nature is happiest when the world around him is ordered and serene.

He is usually not the athletic type, doesn't enjoy participating in or viewing sports. Give him a board game—chess or backgammon or whatever—and watch his interest pick up.

He's a good conversationalist and expects you to keep up with him, so *do* stay alert and bright. If you don't know Picasso from Beethoven, try to bone up.

He is kind, has a strong sense of justice and fair play, and will give anyone an even shake. He is tactful, diplomatic, and has a keen sense of humor. By nature peaceable and loving, he will resent it keenly when an injustice has been committed.

In business he is marvelous at keeping his employees and associates happy. His instinct is for compromise and adjustment, the reconciliation of opposing sides. Because it is hard for him to decide an issue flatly, however, he tends to put off hard decisions. Often he needs a partner who will do the emotionally unpleasant chore—like discharging an incompetent.

In a business dispute, he would prefer to have the issue resolved by an impartial panel of some kind, perhaps a jury. Of course, he'll want to be part of the jury. There is no one who has a better ability to smooth over difficulties, reduce tensions, and placate angry tempers—so the jury can reach the decision he wanted them to reach in the first place.

For this is the crux: Libra man is quite determined to have his way while avoiding the appearance of personal bias or involvement. If things don't go his way, you will suddenly discover beneath his rational, fair, and tolerant exterior a quite different man.

He has highly accurate intuitions, so don't try to deceive him. The only time the wool can be pulled over his eyes is when he's putting on his sweater. He is aware of the reality of things, and when it comes to probing motives, he has X-ray vision.

However, even if he sees through you, he'll try to understand your reasons. And he won't get emotional about it. He hates making a scene.

A man born under this sign loves beauty in architecture, paintings, music, theater—and women. In courtship he wields charm as a weapon. But while he may know most ways to lure a woman, he does have a problem. When she is ready, he's not sure whether to take her or not.

The reason for his indecision is that he is weighing the moment in a delicate balance. Everything must be perfect. The smallest particle of doubt sets him to work again, fussing with her levers and controls. Some girls love it, but they're usually the ones who delight in the exquisiteness of prolonged torture.

Don't lose hope. Let him know how much he turns you on and you'll find him warming to you quickly. If your man was born under the sign of the scales, you've already learned that when you do get him into bed it is a rewarding experience. The Libra male is determined to satisfy his mate—even if it takes all night!

In love, you can count on getting more than an equal shake. He believes sex is a rewarding experience, for both himself and his partner. And he has the patience needed to satisfy. Keep the lights low, and don't be vulgar or coarse. All you have to do is clearly indicate to him what you want when, and how you want it. You'll find him ready and willing to please.

In general: The Libran male responds easily to praise and flattery. You can coax him into almost anything with a few well-chosen compliments. He hates to hurt anyone's feelings, and so is usually at the mercy of an aggressive woman.

He's practically a pushover for a woman who knows what she wants from him. It's almost too easy for him to fall in love, and when he does it's hard for him to get out of the involvement. One reason is that he hates emotionalism. The woman willing to make a scene has virtually won the argument before it starts.

He became interested in girls at an early age—an interest that will continue all his life—but he's also a natural for marriage. It's easy to make him fall in love. However, make all the plans for the wedding and *include him out*. He doesn't like to be bothered with details. They upset him.

He will be happiest if you display an even temper with not too many emotional highs or lows. He finds it a little difficult to differentiate clearly between friendship and love, but he is possessive. *Don't flirt with other men.*

He has a definite affinity toward women who dress well, have long hair, and he prefers lips to be slightly moist. One tip: If your clothes look as though they can easily be removed, he finds that *very* hard to keep out of mind.

HIS SEX LIFE

While it's true that you have to lead the way, do bear in mind that he is eager to please and there is nothing he won't try. He is almost overly concerned about whether you have an orgasm. And he can become quite uninhibited with the right inducement. Do use your fingertips on him. He responds beautifully if you lightly stroke his testicles.

However, don't be impatient. If you try to rush him, he'll simply turn off and lose his erection. Nothing is more calculated to turn a passionate woman into a vexatious and frustrated shrew!

His deliberateness can make for exciting foreplay if you'll simply relax and enjoy it. The combination of art and leisure is likely to leave you completely satiated. He has an intimate knowledge of female anatomy, an active erotic imagination, and all the right intuitions.

Don't be deceived by his usually slight physique. The Libran male has staying power. He's slow, but he's steady, and the odds are that you'll be the first to cry enough!

Basically, he enjoys lovemaking that avoids any suggestion of coarseness. He knows how to caress a woman's body, and by the time he has undressed her she is turned on. In foreplay he is patient, affectionate, and imaginative. What's more, his passions won't push a self-destruct button and disappear in five seconds—not while there is a whole world of wonderful sensation to explore. In the full sexual embrace, he is insistent, forceful, and has more stamina than any woman can ask for.

Sex for him is a rounded experience, not merely a quick tumble between the sheets. Your pleasure is what he has in mind while he's nibbling your breast or sucking your toes, running his tongue in circles under your armpit or along the inside of your thighs. When his fingertips lightly stroke your clitoris he knows just what kind of exquisite little sensations are shooting up into your brain. A favorite technique of the Libra male is to move with light lip caresses to the area between the vulva and the anus. This gentle prodding near the anus is guaranteed to start any woman breathing heavily.

If you are the kind who can relax and enjoy this without some feelings of congestive impatience, more power to you. If you feel that all this foreplay has got to lead to something quickly, then you may have to take control. But do it gently. Beware of trying to order him about in the bedroom.

Forgotten to take the Pill? If there is no other form of contraceptive handy, the Libran will be quite understanding. He doesn't mind being masturbated, having oral sex, or being relieved between your breasts or even clasped in your armpit. Anything that gives you pleasure is likely to give him pleasure! But he wants to know exactly what is expected of him before the fun and frolic begins. On the other hand, he isn't likely to draw the line at anything—as long as he's been told in advance.

He is *not* faithful. Because he doesn't feel deeply, most of his relationships are shallow. He sees nothing wrong with carrying on two or more affairs at the same time.

His tendency toward voyeurism expresses itself in

several ways. He gets pleasure from watching other couples fornicating, whether the other couples are male or female or mixed. He may put a mirror at the proper angle to watch his own lovemaking or ask his love partner to join him in wearing a mask, thereby again creating the illusion of two other people.

He enjoys body painting. He will use a small brush to delicately paint certain areas of his own and his partner's body—with pleasingly erotic results. Some Libra males tape-record their bed sessions and play them back, so no vivid sound will be lost.

He is a connoisseur of refinement, a devotee of exotic varieties of titillation.

Libran male is very attractive to women—more gigolos are born under this sign than any other—and to homosexuals. Because the Libra personality is so finely balanced between the two sexes, he is often bisexual.

His basically easygoing and tolerant nature extends into all matters sexual. If his partner wishes to experiment with another man (or woman), he doesn't mind particularly. He is likely to be found in the middle of a *ménage à trois,* and may very well, like the hero in the movie version of *Cabaret,* be dealing at one and the same time with both other members of the *ménage.*

Because of his frequent voluntary sexual abstinence (he waits until the mood is upon him), he is strongly inclined toward exotic varieties of masturbation. Fairly common among Libra males is masturbation while looking at photographs of women wearing furs and jewels. One Libra man told me that he would take his wife's fox fur with him into the bathroom and tickle his penis with it until he was ready to come. Another liked to enter the bathroom while his girl friend was bathing, stand at the side of the tub, and masturbate directly on her.

Others prefer masturbation with more physical contact, and for this purpose almost anything with a hole, or in which a hole can be made, will do. I've heard of doughnuts, fruits, toilet paper rolls, and sponges. And I'm sure some Libra males could add to this list.

FIRST MOVES

Libra needs to be admired. Don't weigh compliments before delivering them. Hand them over on a silver platter to be gobbled up—but don't make the mistake of being too obvious. You must be sincere and not pay the routine or cliché compliment. (For example, don't make the mistake one man did of telling a beautiful Libran model, who made her living exhibiting her lovely hands on TV commercials, that she had lovely hands. She knew that, and was thoroughly bored.) Compliment a smart man on his physique, a beautiful woman on her intelligence. That way you won't be parroting what's been said a hundred times before.

If you want an opening topic, try a current news item. State your own opinion strongly. Librans may disagree, but never disagreeably. They are far too interested in hearing both sides of the question. One tip: They tend to be on the side of the underdog. They have great sympathy for the underprivileged and the minorities.

Don't forget: Libra loves luxury. If you give a gift, make it a memorable one. Sterling silver, fourteen-carat gold, Lalique crystal, tiny diamonds, French champagne. The Libra woman adores jewelry, especially ornate pieces.

When you go out on a date, don't let the vulgar problem of expense intrude. Take the Libran to a fine restaurant, a show, a concert, an art gallery. Show that you too have good taste.

Consider the ambiance. Librans are strongly responsive to atmosphere. Choose quiet places with subtle, discreet lighting. If you bring him to your apartment for dinner, serve a meal that a gourmet will dote on (even if you have to order it sent up beforehand from a great restaurant!). Make sure that your Libra is surrounded with glamor and "class."

And when the delicious moment arrives, make certain that the surroundings are equal to the occasion. If you can't afford satin sheets and subtle lighting, at least put some thought into the production. Music is an aid. So is champagne. It doesn't have to be all Busby Berkeley, but you must provide a proper setting.

After that, beauty is as beauty does!

EROGENOUS ZONES

The small of the back and the buttocks are the sensitive areas for Librans. On social occasions, dancing, or even strolling together, let your fingers gently caress the lower part of your Libran's back. In more intimate moments, put both hands on Libra's bare buttocks and with the heels of the hands make small circles, tracing a path upward across the small of the back toward the top of the spine. Use moderate pressure, and return to the buttocks for the *coup de grace*. It will drive the true Libran into a frenzy.

If the Libran is a male, he will go mad for the gentle stiff pressure of your nipples against the lower part of his back. You won't have to do it twice.

For all Librans, the buttocks is a highly erogenous zone. Female Libra loves having this area rubbed, fondled, patted, and playfully pinched, and becomes sexually aroused by such attentions. She is also very partial to lovemaking positions where her buttocks are prominently displayed to her lover, such as in rear entry intercourse. Librans of both sexes respond to vigorous assault to their bottoms with bare hand, paddle, or whip. Incidentally, Librans can usually be identified by their especially well-shaped and rounded buttocks.

LAST MOVES

It's easy to get out of the affair. There are so many ways to annoy a Libran.

Put on weight, become sloppy in dress, make your dates in crowded, noisy places, talk about inane subjects, begin to pick arguments.

Complain about their extravagance with money. Insist on handling financial affairs yourself to check their spending.

Nag them about keeping appointments and making deadlines.

Open their mail. Librans consider this particular invasion of privacy to be gross and unforgivable.

Stop paying compliments. Prepare TV dinners. Let soiled sheets stay on the bed. When you're making love, try to hurry things up. What's the point of all this fussing around?

Be hypercritical. If they respond in their usual tolerant way, tell them their minds are so open their brains are likely to fall out.

Complain about their cooking. Librans—male and female—pride themselves on their skill in the culinary art. Tell them how they have just met their Waterloo in the Beef Wellington.

If the denouement is taking too long because you've worked too deeply into his or her graces to shake yourself loose, there's one sure way. In the middle of the next argument, get a little physical. The threat alone will probably suffice. You'll end up talking to the wall.

Your Libran will have left *you.*

YOUR SENSUAL GUIDE

LIBRA and ARIES: This relationship suffers from an underlying tension. Aries is aggressive and restless, while Libra seeks perfection and needs peaceful companions. The basic disparity of temperament leads to inevitable quarrels. However, the sexual relationship should be good. Fine bedroom, poor living room is the prognosis. That adds up to a likely affair, and a quite unlikely marriage.

LIBRA and TAURUS: Taurus is too possessive and earthy for romantic Libra. Libra may soon have a very jealous mate on its hands. However, they are physically in tune and that helps. Libra is considerate, understanding, and will cope with Taurus's temper and stubbornness. A tendency toward fickleness in Libra might drive Taurus wild. Fun and games, but longer odds against a durable union.

LIBRA and GEMINI: Both find it difficult to restrict their affections. Love can make the world go around—but this pair gives it a shove. Except for this one problem, however, theirs is an ideal mating. Both are passionate, neither is particularly jealous or possessive. They share many personality traits and are great company in bed. A fine affair, and a warm and happy marriage.

LIBRA and CANCER: Cancer can be overcritical, particularly about Libra's extravagance. Cancer likes to stay close to home; Libra likes to wander. Cancer is practical and thrifty; Libra is impulsive and likes what money will buy. Not much compatibility here. Deeply affectionate, trusting Cancer will be shocked by Libra's shallow emotions and inconstancy. A tolerable affair, an intolerable marriage.

* * *

LIBRA and LEO: These two supply each other's wants and needs. Leo is passionate, Libra demonstrative—and both are hooked on sex. It will be shooting stars all the way in the bedroom. If egos clash, Libra must yield however. That won't be too difficult, for Libra is usually cooperative. Strategy and tact are Libra's weapons. A torrid affair can become a pretty warm marriage too.

LIBRA and VIRGO: Virgo lives by the rule book and that is not Libra's way. And there are other personality pitfalls. Virgo is a pinchpenny who may be more interested in finances than in sex. Libra finds this unforgivable. Virgo can also be nagging and critical, even dictatorial. Libra will resent this and start looking elsewhere for appreciation. A dubious affair, a most difficult marriage.

LIBRA and LIBRA: They respond to each other with equal passion. They have much in common. They are gay, social, affectionate, and love harmony and beauty. But when the first blush is over, hard reality intrudes. Neither of this pair wants to come down out of the clouds. Their lovemaking may take on ho-hum overtones. An affair should work, a marriage requires maturity and a more practical attitude.

LIBRA and SCORPIO: Scorpio is too jealous for easygoing Libra. Scorpio's justifiably renowned jealousy won't put up with even minor flirtations. Libra's casual manner toward sex keeps Scorpio seething. Scorpio must dominate, Libra must cooperate. There is a good deal of physical magnetism, but a magnetic field can build to an explosion. A passionate, stormy affair. Marriage likewise.

* * *

LIBRA and SAGITTARIUS: Sagittarius has a strong penchant for adventure and will never bore Libra. Libra's flirtations will leave Sagittarius only tolerant and amused. Both are sexually well mated. The problem lies in Sagittarius's reluctance to settle down and need for independence. Libra wants a real partnership and a pleasant home base. If they can work out these differences, auguries are fine for either a short- or long-term relationship.

LIBRA and CAPRICORN: Capricorn has a strong physical attraction for Libra, who also finds Capricorn's knack for making money useful. But Libra's lazy ways offend Capricorn's nose-to-the-grindstone attitude. And Libra is frustrated by Capricorn's sober practicality. Capricorn won't like Libra's socializing. Too many personality conflicts here for a successful marriage. An affair will be shortlived.

LIBRA and AQUARIUS: These two should get along famously. Libra looks to Aquarius for leadership in adventurous living. They enjoy socializing and will become involved in public affairs. They have many friends but also feel free to pursue their own special interests. And they will make love beautifully—even if they forget to make the bed! A sexy affair, and fine auguries for a stimulating marriage.

LIBRA and PISCES: A complicated combination. Pisces's gentleness, sensitivity, and devotion are what Libra likes. However, Pisces is not a dominant sign and Libra is unwilling to supply the firm leadership required. Libra begins to resent Pisces's cloying dependency, and Pisces disapproves of Libra's many other interests. When Libra turns into a scold or a nitpicker, Pisces wallows in misery. Sad? Yes, for any serious affair and a marriage also.

SCORPIO

October 23–November 21

THE FEMALE

She could write a book about how to walk and talk and look—when enticing a man. This smoldering voluptuary dwells in the valley of her desires and is dedicated to the satisfaction of her body's yearnings. Only a low-sexed male fails to respond to the slumbering passion in her eyes and voice. Without speaking a syllable, she can spell sex in all the known human dialects.

When she meets an attractive man, she knows just how to cut him out of the herd, and it isn't long before he is too dazzled to notice any other woman. He will be well advised not to struggle. It will be no contest—a case of an irresistible force against a highly movable object. Even if she isn't good-looking, her large hypnotic eyes will fix him with a dominating stare. He'll know just how the poor hare feels when hypnotized by a cobra.

She resents a stingy escort. Wherever she goes, she likes to travel first class, and you'd better pay up with a smile. If you are a little taken aback by her casual way with money, don't show it. Or you and your money will soon be forgotten.

She has enough energy for several women. She likes to work and play hard. In any kind of activity she tends toward excess. That can be fascinating but exhausting. You'll never be bored, but you may pine for a more quiet, placid life.

She takes love seriously. Like the male of the species, she is a creature of her passions. But this does not always relate directly to sex; her passion for life exists independent of any man. This makes her irresistible to men, who would like to subdue her and make her dependent. Even when they succeed, they are unlikely to penetrate the secret depths of her hidden sensuality.

In the bedroom she is demanding, and her standards of performance are hard for many men to meet. She has little patience for those who don't measure up or leave her feeling short-changed. On the other hand, she is most efficient with those who merely suffer from psychological inhibitions, and can and will perform wonders for the impotent male—if his impotence is in his mind. This isn't altruism on her part. The way she looks at it, she's simply doing what's necessary to help *him* satisfy *her*.

She has a shrewd mind and is gifted with remarkable intuition. Overly critical and exacting, she subjects both would-be friends and lovers to a prolonged scrutiny before accepting them into her scheme of life. She sees deep into other people's motivations, while remaining impenetrable to their probings. Her real character is not easy to discern and may always remain her secret.

She is stubborn about getting her way. And she has the patience and ability to dissimulate to achieve her goals. All her moves are planned carefully to reach her objective. It takes a powerful will and real determination to resist her, for she knows what she wants and will press toward it with unremitting force. She cannot be diverted, nor will she adapt to changing circumstances.

Warning: Her intense emotional nature, if frustrated, can become vengeful and destructive. Betrayed, she makes a most dangerous enemy. Hell hath no fury like a Scorpio scorned. She has no scruples in seeking revenge on one who has been unworthy of her trust. She wants not only to punish the offender but to humiliate and degrade him.

Jealousy is her worst fault. She expects her lover to reserve all his admiration for her. She finds rivals and intrigues where none are to be found. At a party, if her escort spends a few minutes in private conversation with an attractive female, she decides that he's arranging a secret rendezvous—and acts accordingly. And she isn't the type to stand by quietly in a corner pretending to be a lamp. She will descend in full ravening fury.

She despises weakness or anyone who crumples under pressure. For such types she has all the compassion of a middle linebacker. If there's an opening in your defenses, she'll find it. And if you want to stay close to her, you must be able to "take it," because she can dish it out.

Favorably disposed, she treats a lover royally. But when her mood changes (and it will), she flays him to the bone. Her quarrels are always at a high-decibel rating. If you haven't made up the quarrel before parting, don't call the next day as if nothing had happened. You'll feel as though you're talking to a complete stranger on a crossed telephone line.

One thing you can be sure of: She is deeply emotional, highly sensitive, and fiercely loyal to the one she loves. She will make great sacrifices for anyone who really engages her affections. If a man meets her halfway, she will be his forever.

Scorpio women make loyal mistresses who will defend you in public, fight for you in the most adverse conditions, and scorn what the neighbors say or think. But don't whine or weaken, for then she can turn on you.

Marriage? As you've probably guessed by now, it can be heaven or hell. There is no middle road. Remember—this is the most extreme sign of the zodiac. She's a formidable woman. Faint hearts had better steer clear.

HER SEX LIFE

A long night ahead, fellows. Pace yourselves.

She may begin by whispering provocative obscenities into your ear. Merely talking about sex moves her toward orgasm. She's the one who insists on that oversized waterbed or one of the large round beds that have neither head nor foot and so accommodate any position with comfort. She's an activist in the bedroom. She will do anything to make the night memorable.

She is inquisitive, searching, and experimental. No matter how jaded you are about sexual procedures, some of her impetuous actions will surprise you. She wants you to enjoy sex as much as she does, and she enjoys it with an intensity that approaches the ecstatic. This is the sexiest sign in the zodiac.

Erotic, demanding, she requires a mate of equal ardor for complete fulfillment. The clinical approach, however, is not for her. Her behavior is guided wholly by instinct. No book will ever convince her that sex is merely a system of yoga exercises. She would rather go to bed with even a bad lover than with a good book.

She is a caress for any man's ego. When she is excited physically, she shows it, and this in turn will fire his passions. She likes to keep making love for a long time, and is able to impose her own wishes on an otherwise too quickly impulsive male. For she knows that eroticism consists of much, much more than the mere physical act of lovemaking. Even the most minute details are important, and she will make him fully aware of their importance.

Look for her to show up in the sheerest panties or the kind that are open right at the crotch for extra titillation and convenience. Or she will wear a French bra with no cups or a black garter belt. Scorpio woman may look like a perfect lady on the outside, but she will dress, and behave, like an abandoned whore in the privacy of the bedroom. When a man interests her, she will pursue him with determination and guile, and she *never* takes no for an answer.

During the sex act, control of orgasm is very important to her, and she will try any method to help her man maintain his potency. Nupercaine or other nerve deadeners on the tip of his penis will subdue the urgent sensations that bring on a climax too quickly, and this is a tactic I have found to be a favorite among Scorpio women.

In the course of long experience, I have met many who use dildoes, single and double and rectal. They also like scented body oils, flavored lubricating gels, and twelve-inch vibrators. She is not subtle in her assault on her goal—and her goal is always her own sexual pleasure.

Once a Scorpio woman is turned on, the difficulty is in turning her off. She wants more than you have to give and has ways to make you give more. It might be the insertion of a dildo or a vibrator in the anus during intercourse or a thrust of the vibrator to massage the prostate. *That's* an experience you won't soon forget!

She'll be very unhappy if she gets the idea that you're reluctant to cooperate. Scorpio woman intends to dominate her male partner. Not long ago I had a letter from a man having an affair with a Scorpio woman. At first intrigued by her extreme ideas on how to copulate, he had now begun to get worried. For their latest encounter, she had donned a costume of skintight leather from head to foot and wore fantastic high heels shaped like large spikes. She had walked on his bare back with her shoes, then forced him to kiss her leather uniform, lick it and fondle it. All this before she even let him make love to her!

The poor fellow wanted to know how to turn her off before she progressed to a cat-o'-nine-tails. I told him that his chance of changing Scorpio woman's ways were nearly nil, and the best thing to do was to leave her. (I knew he wouldn't, for he was Pisces!)

This urge to dominate sometimes takes lesbian forms even with a male partner. Over the years I have encountered Scorpio women who said they liked nothing better than to strap a dildo about their waists and "rape" a man. One particularly aggressive female told me that first she used the handle of a whip to "stimulate" his rectum.

In their need for more complaisant and passive partners, Scorpio females drift into lesbian affairs. In lesbian intercourse, the dominant Scorpio, when not using a dildo, favors the "spoon" position in which anal intercourse or coitus is simulated from the rear. Most of the sexual play is very similar to heterosexuality, and the Scorpio female usually behaves in a masculine fashion not only during the sexual performances but in other areas of the relationship.

Whatever the method, Scorpio woman will command her sexual partner to do what she wants—far beyond the ordinary call of duty. For her, sex is just another expression of the master-slave relationship, and Scorpio must always be master!

THE MALE

The man born under the sign of Scorpio is ruled by his genitalia. He is passionate, emotional, unpredictable. His nature is governed by his desires, and to satisfy them he will accept any challenge, confront any obstacle. Nor will he reckon the consequences. Let others label him a heartless Don Juan; their opinion will not inhibit his restless search for sexual adventure.

It isn't hard to understand why people are drawn to him like steel filings to a magnet. They respond to his almost hypnotic sensuality. He combines in equal measure charm and strength of character. He seems to have so much energy that he actually exudes it into the atmosphere; it surrounds him like a nimbus wherever he goes.

But there is danger for a woman in getting too close to a Scorpio male. His smoldering sexuality can explode without notice. Volatile, unpredictable, he makes little effort at self-control. Restraint is not a word that can be found in his vocabulary. If you want to flirt with danger without suffering the consequences, stay away from this fellow. High Voltage is written all over him.

Lovemaking with him can rise to great heights of passion or descend into the most depraved acts. A woman who becomes the desired love partner of a Scorpio male has either much to look forward to or much to fear. Nothing will stop her man from achieving his goal, for he is a victim of his desires. In mutual love play, he can be an ardent mate who revels in anything that will excite her. If she is unwilling to be wooed and won, he will literally do anything, take any risk, make every move that will persuade her to yield to him. And if all else fails—rape!

Scorpio never forgets a kindness, never forgives an injury, and if wounded his one aim becomes *vengeance!* His relations with people usually involve some element of struggle and strife, and at times he can become violent. He makes enemies all too easily—but let his enemies beware. In any conflict he is an adversary to beware of. He is fierce, headstrong, and tenacious. Those who deal with a Scorpio male must be prepared to make extraordinary efforts to maintain the peace. The tender quality of mercy is not in his makeup, and the way of compromise is not his. If you start trouble with him, be prepared to go to the limit. Because you'll have to. When challenged, Scorpio fights literally to the death. In an argument he will put everything at risk, gambling for all or nothing, and let the devil take the loser.

His motivations appear complex and mysterious, for he has a hidden and private side to his personality. He is dynamic and overbearing but loyal to friends. He does not wish to become dependent but needs someone to lean on. Unstable emotionally, he despises weakness in others—but has great appeal for masochistic types who sense his capacity for cruelty and degeneracy.

He tends to waste his energy in dissipation, in the headlong pursuit of pleasure, and he often becomes addicted to alcohol or drugs. However, his chances of conquering the addiction are better than others', for he is possessed of enormous will power and determination.

Work is important to him. Although he dislikes hard physical labor, he has unusual powers of concentration, a vivid imagination, great courage and enterprise—attributes that usually spell success. He is also practical in matters of finance. No one will ever persuade him to make change for a three-dollar bill.

A drawback is that he likes to blitz a problem, then forget about it. That sometimes leaves the problem not entirely solved.

In affairs of the heart, he simply won't take no for an answer. He expects you to commit yourself wholly to him and his needs. If you don't, he will be ruthless about cutting the ties that bind.

Those born under this sign can be cunning, selfish, and unscrupulous, and these traits are in evidence when they look for sexual adventure. In their view, passion is a law unto itself! Among Scorpio you find the most reckless sex fiends, the most insatiable copulators. They strive for mastery, for complete control over the libido and the emotions.

To the Scorpio male sex is a game in which he has

calculated all the odds and has maximum chances for success. He may enjoy the chase but is only interested in the woman that everyone else wants.

You can drive a Scorpio wild with jealousy—but you do so at your own risk. Domineering with women, confident of his power to compel them to perform his will, his strong wayward passions can lead him toward brutality.

In a word, he's a handful.

Beware!

HIS SEX LIFE

He's a lustful sexy animal. In bed, count on getting more than you bargained for. He has an intimate knowledge of female anatomy and an active erotic imagination. No holds are barred, and no prudery is allowed to interfere.

Every encounter must produce the maximum amount of delight. His energies are insatiable. He will start off on a high note and continue on an ascending scale. From the first kiss you know that he means business. He will go straight for his objective.

He isn't concerned with refinements of technique. All he wants to do is satisfy the uncontrollable imperious demands of his genitalia. Before he finishes undressing, he is ready to go. His compulsive need is all too evident when he stands there naked, legs apart. That turns on a woman, too. In fact, she will usually be panting with welcome before he enters her. One woman I know described making love with a Scorpio lover as "something like watching an avalanche come your way!"

He comes on strong. His kisses are not sweet pecks, but fierce rough male caresses. He enjoys biting and sucking, and is a past master at cunnilingus. Inflicting pain turns him on. During foreplay he may pinch the nipples or the inside of your thighs, insert his thumb into your vagina and his middle finger into the anus and then snap his fingers on the thin membrane (the perineum). This can cause tremendous erotic sensations along with the pain.

His need is to completely dominate a woman. If she will bear pain from him, that signifies her submission. He indulges himself in the fantasy that most women like to be sexually assaulted, physically overpowered.

Ruled by his genitalia, he enjoys having a lover worship at the throne. A tongue running over his penis, sucking, taking little nips, makes him throb with response. He particularly likes to meet you coming from a hot tub, let you fellate him, then press your warm moist naked body back against cool wall tiles and enter standing up. Wetness appeals to him (Scorpio is a water sign), and his sense of sexual urgency is satisfied by the quick union of naked bodies. He'll want to continue in the bedroom (Scorpio is *always* willing to continue), or he may put you back in the tub for an encore. Tip: You'd better have quick and easy access to the vaginal creams and jellies that lessen the soreness from returning so often to the fray.

Scorpio will go to unusual lengths to add pleasure to his couplings. One man I recall invariably masturbated before having intercourse; another bit his lips until they bled or pinched himself severely so that pain would temporarily halt his orgasm. One particularly interesting fellow told me he had discovered how to strengthen his penis muscles while urinating—simply halting and starting the flow every few seconds. As a result, he assured me, women were absolutely delighted during intercourse with his prolonged spurts of sexual potency.

Scorpio male prefers making love when there is some chance of a conception, so he is excited by women who do not use contraceptives. He doesn't like to use condoms or such male contraceptive methods as coitus interruptus, in which the penis is withdrawn just before ejaculation. One method Scorpio will use is to bathe his testicles in hot water before intercourse, which sometimes achieves a temporary infertility. (It is a fact that the testicles are located outside the body because the sperm manufactured therein cannot live even in the body heat of 98.6 degrees.) A reason Scorpio male prefers this method is the pleasure-pain stimulation it gives to the genitalia.

One thing I have never found: a Scorpio male who asks me questions about how to enjoy better sex. That is not surprising to anyone who understands those born under the sign of the Scorpion. To ask questions would somehow indicate sexual ignorance or inferiority—and no true Scorpio would ever be guilty of that! Sex is far too serious a business.

Scorpio male is prone to kinkiness. He enjoys far-out sex and experiments with anything that will make the experience memorable. One of the least kinky is to make it larger and harder. Males born under this sign also tend to favor the more sophisticated type of dildoes—the new kind of artificial penises that exude warmth, ejaculate a semenlike substance, and even have built-in vibrators!

His latent violence can turn real and vicious. He has a strong tendency toward the paranoid when he feels he's being denied.

Scorpio derives pleasure from someone else's pain, and this leads easily into sadistic practices. Not long ago, newspaper accounts told of a man who had set up a dungeon in his basement where he brought girls to torture them before possessing them. He hung a victim by her arms, clamped her to the wall with ropes and chains, and gagged her with a handball and a cord that made it difficult for her to breathe. I don't need the confirmation of the sadist's birth date to recognize the signature of Scorpio!

For less obviously criminal types, there are milder forms of Scorpio obsession. He prefers coarse wood tables and hard floors to silk sheets and satin pillows. He likes to drive a woman to multiple—and I mean *multiple*—orgasms, usually with the aid of electrical stimulation. It works this way: He straps a vibrator to his hand and, taking the clitoris between thumb and index fingers, lets the gentle surging motion bring her to orgasm after orgasm. Sometimes he varies the procedure by inserting two fingers in the vagina before throwing the switch on the vibrator or puts only the index finger in and his thumb on the clitoris. This kind of pleasure quickly becomes almost unendurable—and nothing pleases Scorpio male more than intermingling pleasure with pain.

FIRST MOVES

I once said that there are only two astrologers in the world who understand Scorpio—and unfortunately they disagree. That was said in jest. It is not really true. I meant to emphasize the unpredictability of those born under this sign, not the impossibility of dealing with them.

There are definite guidelines to follow with Scorpio. First, take them seriously. Their pride responds to the flattery of undivided attention. No matter what Scorpio says, don't set yourself too forcefully against it. That doesn't mean you should be a hypocrite. Scorpio has remarkable intuitive powers, bordering on the occult, and can penetrate your real thoughts.

Nonetheless, they are very susceptible to compliments and won't balk at the most obvious flattering kind—even if they are not deceived by it. Don't stint on the remarks about how she dresses (which is usually in a provocative, flamboyant manner designed to get attention), how pretty she is, or how clever a conversationalist. When he makes a joke, laugh, because he'll be offended if you don't. Try to overlook his faults. In fact, try to regard them as virtues: i.e., "I like a man who knows his own mind," "I've never seen anyone win an argument with you," or "You're so thoroughly *masculine*, darling."

Don't suggest going to the theater or for a long drive or to a really swinging party. Scorpio loves home too much. Try an evening of sitting in, listening to favorite records, and you'll make better progress.

Always ask for advice. *Never* suggest that anything should be done that Scorpio dislikes. You have to go more than halfway to keep the relationship on an even keel. Accept the premise that Scorpio knows *everything* a little better than *anybody*, and you're well on your way into Scorpio's affections.

Be affectionate. Scorpio needs a lot of affection and will repay in kind.

Above all, pay exclusive attention to any Scorpio, male or female, for otherwise they will become resentful and jealous. And go along with any Scorpio plan. They don't like to be crossed and will allow for only small amendments to their stated purpose.

When dating a Scorpio woman, be a free spender. If she invites you to dinner, be sure you bring a bottle of expensive, vintage champagne.

When trying to attract Scorpio male, be provocative. Wear clothes that show off your figure, put on your most tantalizing perfume. Remember that you can't be coy with Scorpio.

Gift-giving? For male or female, try a piece of exotic jewelry, like a Mexican or African amulet. Scorpios love to adorn their bodies. Give her something sensuous and daring to wear in a bold crimson color. Give him boots in black leather or a striking jeweled belt. Once the affair with a Scorpio man is underway, give him a band of pure gold to wear around his penis. It's the newest fad in men's jewelry and perfectly suited for sexy Scorpio. For a Scorpio woman, try topaz earrings. The topaz is Scorpio's lucky gem, and heavy dangling earrings cause a subliminal erotic excitement when they brush against her neck. You can always take them off her ears and rub them gently on her clitoris. A jeweled treat for a very sexy lady.

Small tip: When having dinner out, suggest a seafood restaurant. Favorite food for Scorpio is lobster—and you'll win points by letting him or her nibble at a claw.

It will help Scorpio's romantic mood if the atmosphere is seductive. Spread some floor cushions, burn incense, play romantic records. Not that ambiance is all that important. In the final analysis, Scorpio will also make love on the cement floor of a garage full of gasoline fumes and roaring car engines.

EROGENOUS ZONES

The most sensitive area for Scorpio is the genitalia. For the male, even a light fingering in the genital area will turn him into a volcano. And why not? He gets a charge just out of wearing jockey shorts over boxer shorts! The female of this sign can rouse herself just by crossing her legs and moving them while in this position so that her "lips" rub together. (Some other approaches to sensitive areas of Scorpio anatomy have already been discussed.)

Nothing under heaven pleases Scorpio male more than a light flicking of a woman's tongue on the head of his penis. Do I have to add that Scorpio woman takes a particular delight in cunnilingus?

When you fool around with Scorpio's genitalia, you literally have your partner in the palm of your hand!

LAST MOVES

The way out of an affair can be dangerous. Scorpio has a bad temper, and a head-on confrontation may prove disastrous. Better to use more subtle methods.

Taper off on the affection Scorpio so badly needs. Don't bother with the usual hugging, kissing, or verbal assurances of love.

Put your own interests first. Complain that you don't get enough attention. Brood and sulk. Point out frequently, and precisely, what they have done wrong on any social occasion.

Monopolize conversations, even when you don't really know what you're talking about.

In the bedroom, don't let him or her have everything their own way.

Never praise them.

If you're a woman trying to break with Scorpio male, be a lousy housekeeper and let the house fall apart. Invite people to the house for a party and choose the kind of boisterous guests who are likely to tear up "the nest" a little.

If you're a male, drop ashes everywhere, scatter your clothes and newspapers, leave dirty finger marks on the walls. Letting Scorpio's home deteriorate is almost as unforgivable as doubting Scorpio's infallibility!

Make Scorpio jealous, then laugh at their possessiveness—and go right on doing what you're doing. If they demand an explanation, offer the kind that could be put between covers and published as fiction.

Scorpio won't stick around any longer than a purse snatcher.

But remember—never argue! You may break up the relationship, but you may also depart on a stretcher!

YOUR SENSUAL GUIDE

SCORPIO and ARIES: A highly volatile combination. In sex, Aries is innovative and Scorpio provides enthusiastic cooperation. But Aries is too happy-go-lucky for jealous Scorpio. Both are self-centered, dynamic, and ambitious. The attraction between them may be strong, but individualism tends to pull them apart. Indications point to a short affair, a rocky long-term relationship.

SCORPIO and TAURUS: Both have the stamina and the passion to satisfy each other in bed. But their personality differences will have to be ironed out if they're to keep liking each other in the morning. Scorpio scorns laziness and is basically thrifty. Taurus is indolent and likes to spend the money it earns. Both are proud, stubborn, domineering. Their strong sexual urges indicate a possible affair. Marriage is extremely dubious.

SCORPIO and GEMINI: Sexually they get along, but that's not the whole story. Concessions on both sides are necessary. Gemini takes everything too lightly for intense Scorpio. Scorpio is determined, while Gemini is changeable and shifting. Gemini is intellectually keen and enjoys showing off on any social occasion; Scorpio considers that a hideous waste of time. A fluctuating affair, a difficult marriage.

SCORPIO and CANCER: These two water signs should get along very well. The sexual prognosis is also good: Scorpio's passion finds a willing partner in Cancer. Physical compatibility helps to reduce the jealous traits from which both signs suffer. If flare-ups do occur, however, this is no place for an innocent bystander. For the most part, a harmonious union of strength and protectiveness. Good affair, fine marriage.

SCORPIO and LEO: Both signs are on a short fuse, and the explosive disagreements might end in violence. Passion runs high here. They are physically attracted to each other, but Scorpio cannot give the attention and respect that Leo needs. Leo's pride will be hurt, and in many situations Scorpio's jealous possessiveness will be wounded. Perhaps an exciting liaison, but a horrendous long-term amour.

SCORPIO and VIRGO: Their interests are similar in many areas, but the sexual sphere is not one of them. This makes it hard for them to work out a relationship. Virgo may turn carping, and Scorpio will be brutally frank. If Virgo can make necessary adjustments, it might work. A meeting of minds for a while, but Scorpio will soon start looking for other sexual outlets.

SCORPIO and LIBRA: Scorpio is too possessive and too jealous for Libra; Libra is too lazy and too sensitive for Scorpio. However, they are both passionate (although Libra is on-again, off-again). And they will take seriously the responsibility of living together. There will be a problem about Libra's love of luxury, which Scorpio may not be able to supply. Stormy weather during an affair. Marriage won't be smooth sailing either.

SCORPIO and SCORPIO: Sexually these two could start a fire going underwater. But they are much too alike. Both are determined, possessive, jealous, and have terrible tempers. When they differ, the crockery will start to fly—and the relationship will fly out the window. Their initial intense attraction can't survive outside the heated environs of the bedroom. A *wow* affair, but marriage—*whew!*

* * *

SCORPIO and SAGITTARIUS: Don't bring an expensive house-warming gift to these two. Scorpio loves its home, but Sagittarius has a bag packed and is ready to go. Sagittarius must have freedom; Scorpio is overly possessive and demanding. Not even the Sagittarian sense of humor can bridge the chasm that will open between them. Their only attraction is sex, and that won't last. For a night, yes. For a lifetime, no.

SCORPIO and CAPRICORN: Both are willing, ambitious, and get along well sexually. There should be a minimum of problems. Scorpio tends to be more emotional, which is good for Capricorn's brooding and inward nature. Capricorn welcomes the security that is implied in Scorpio's possessiveness. Scorpio doesn't mind sex without sentiment, and that suits Capricorn too. A warm affair, a strong marriage.

SCORPIO and AQUARIUS: Scorpio abhors Aquarius's changing moods. Aquarius is involved in many social projects outside the home which is where Scorpio's interests lie. Scorpio can't dominate Aquarius, which prizes its liberty too much. Aquarius is very social, Scorpio is not at all. Scorpio has no use for Aquarius's impractical scheming. Bed acrobatics can't keep this disparate couple together. Let them go their separate ways.

SCORPIO and PISCES: This couple has a strong fascination for each other. Pisces will depend on Scorpio's strength to bolster its indecisiveness and will positively revel in Scorpio's possessiveness and dominance. Their sex life should be exciting—Pisces is imaginative, Scorpio is persevering. For either an affair or a marriage, you should have it so good.

SAGITTARIUS

November 22–December 21

THE FEMALE

She's the Dona Juana of the zodiac. She is broad-minded in her choice of lovers. A man may attract her for a particular trait—his enthusiasm, or his ready sense of humor—and she will overlook his other less desirable qualities. She will go from one sexual exploit to another with an easygoing approach, so that everyone remains on a friendly basis.

However, she is not capable of deep emotional involvement and is more likely to follow the caprice of romantic inclination. She is a gambler at the game of love. Each new lover is a roulette chip she tosses onto what she hopes will be a lucky number. Should an affair go sour, she is philosophical. There'll be another lover along in a little while; why weep for a lost love?

She is vain. At the approach of maturity she is likely to take off for the nearest plastic surgeon. One Sagittarius woman I know went to a famous Brazilian surgeon's clinic and, while spending several weeks there recuperating—her face most of the time in bandages—had several love affairs!

Sagittarian woman wants to entertain and be entertained. If things get boring, she'd probably cut her throat just to have something interesting to talk about.

She wears her heart on her sleeve. She is straightforward and honest—also good-natured and generous. She loves her freedom and *must* be free to travel. She needs constant variety and stimulation. Even when she's happy, she can't be happy alone. She needs an audience to witness her happiness.

Basically, the woman born under this sign is willing to explore sex with a promising partner but is far more interested in friendship, the exchange of ideas, and romantic adventure. She can be a tease, however, and it's sometimes difficult for a man to figure out whether she's making a sexual overture or just looking for a friend. "Why can't we just be friends?" was probably first said by a Sagittarian female. *Nothing* can cool off careless rapture more quickly than a question like that!

She never seems to settle into a place. Her apartment usually looks as if she is either just moving in or just moving out. She will quickly move on from a job or a man that doesn't interest her. There is always something else to do, so why be bored?

She's an ideal companion for living with on a day-to-day basis. When Arnold Bennett, the famous English writer, said that the trouble with a permanent arrangement like marriage is its "*dailyness,*" he was not describing life with a Sagittarius woman. Her enthusiasm, cooperativeness, hearty sense of humor, and quick wit are a joy to any man.

She is also a good listener, a good comrade for a man who likes sports and outdoor adventure, and a marvelous social hostess who enlivens any party and who always attracts to her the most fascinating people. What more could the most churlish male ask for?

Before you stop reading this and go off looking for a Sagittarius woman to set up light housekeeping with, consider this: She is a tease, an irreformable flirt. And she turns off many admirers by appearing to "know it all." Most annoying is that usually she really hasn't learned enough about a subject to warrant even the appearance of knowing it all.

Her frankness in affairs of the heart mystifies men. She doesn't check her impulse to talk about other men she has known, and when she's disappointed in a lover she won't hesitate to say so.

Perhaps it's not surprising that many Sagittarian women end up as spinsters!

Her impatient, impulsive nature is always at war with her best interests. She'd do better in life if she had some understanding of her real strengths and weaknesses. But she's the kind who will always leap twice before she looks and will never accept advice or warning from others.

Though she seems quite capable of handling her own affairs, this is deceptive. When she really loves a man, she becomes quite dependent. If he leaves her, she has a tendency to fall apart emotionally.

Thin-skinned and easily humiliated, she is a sucker for flattery. A smooth talker can easily win her over. As a result, she is often victimized by unscrupulous men while Mr. Right gets away. Immature and self-conscious, flighty and changeable, she is hard to understand. And nearly impossible to control.

HER SEX LIFE

Sagittarian woman's favorite sex playground is the outdoors. She will freak out making love in a tent, in a camper, or on a sandy beach. One Sagittarian woman I know liked to drive out with her date on a lonely country road and then make love on the roof of the car. (Fortunately, it wasn't a convertible!) Perhaps this affinity for the outdoors is one reason so many women born under this sign join nudist camps.

She enjoys sex, but don't prolong the preliminaries Her prime interest is in her own gratification. While she doesn't mind foreplay, she prefers to start the main show as soon as possible. She is capable of multiple, if shallow, orgasms.

Some men consider her bed manners tactless, and it's true that she can be very inconsiderate to a lover. If he doesn't give her what she wants, she'll just masturbate while he looks on, unfulfilled.

She likes to tease a partner to a point where he loses control. This is often achieved by a stop-and-start technique. After having aroused a lover nearly to climax by fellating him, she will position herself directly over his erect penis and slowly lower herself onto it. As he reaches the peak of unbearable sensation, she will lift herself off again. She doesn't mind if the man comes too quickly. She will squeeze her vaginal muscles around his penis and "milk" him for further sensations. And then she'll start getting ready for another try. After all, you don't always make it the first time. Lindbergh had to bail out of four different planes before he finally flew one across the Atlantic!

She enjoys the post-coital period in which she can lie with her lover, smoke a cigarette or sip a glass of wine, and talk over the fun they've just had. Sex is a friendly act—and she doesn't dig lovers who behave as if the whole universe had just been changed.

Her basic difficulty is her inability to give herself fully to any one experience. She indiscriminately flits from one to another, never offering much resistance and never finding much satisfaction either. She has too many experiences with too little real feeling.

Unlike her male counterpart, the Sagittarian female is not turned on by experimentation. She has no interest in French ticklers, electric vibrators, or tasty douche sprays. These exotic bedroom toys don't fascinate her. She is no connoisseur of erotica. She definitely prefers the "tried and true" forms of sex play and doesn't care to branch out into variations that she considers mere excess.

Recently, a Sagittarian woman in her mid-forties came to me for a consultation. Her problem was that, while she had rushed into an affair with a handsome younger man, she had no desire to continue with the kind of sex tricks he wanted. Apparently, her lover was urging her to such activities as planting a banana in her vagina and then using her muscles to raise and lower it so that he could eat it without using his hands. Not unnaturally, being a Sagittarius, she found such excesses very distasteful. (Need I add that he was a Scorpio?) I agreed that this was not the kind of fruit salad that made for a happy or enduring relationship.

Sagittarius's liberated sexual attitudes do lead her into circumstances where she will make love to women as well as men—and often both together. In a lesbian affair, she is usually the aggressive "butch." For some reason, in such relationships she is often cruel and sadistic. At the very least, she is solely intent on satisfying her own sexual craving. With a lesbian partner she usually favors the use of a double dildo—a dildo with two heads, one end inserted into each woman's vagina.

She doesn't necessarily restrict herself to *Homo sapiens*. Because she is very fond of animals, her indiscriminate affections can turn to bestiality. She particularly likes dogs and horses—or anything else she can tame. Xaviera Hollander describes such an episode in her best-seller, *The Happy Hooker*, and, while no reader surveys have been made, part of the book's popularity can certainly be attributed to the erotic stimulation her description gave to the repressed desires of a multitude of Sagittarian women!

THE MALE

You'll feel more alive the minute you meet him. He's gay, charming, witty, and will convey the impression that you are the most interesting woman he's ever met.

Don't be deceived. If you look closely, you'll see his eyes dance from female to female in the room. The truth is he wants them all!

When a pretty woman enters the room, he will follow her, refreshing her drink, offering her party tidbits, showering her with attention, trying everything in his repertoire to dazzle her. He will get her address and telephone number, besiege her with phone calls, candy, flowers, and other gifts.

In romance he is an idealist who thinks that the very next girl will be The One. No matter how many times he is disappointed, his optimism survives. He regards every new day as a new opportunity—after all, it's a day he's never seen before. It can be exciting just to wake up and discover it is Tuesday.

He is a sentimentalist, with a heart practically asking to be pierced—like a boil. He wants to be in love but is wary of alliances. No affair is going to last long, for it is his nature to create problems when there are none. Then his analytical nature takes over and breaks the problem down in a way that proves it cannot be solved.

He fights against a close involvement and detests jealousy in a woman. What he prefers are liaisons with women who have some experience, for they are likely to take amour as lightly as he does. He would as soon please her as be pleased himself, and he believes in mixing romance with a sense of humor.

Actually, he is not prepared to enter into a long-lasting, truly intimate relationship. He treats amour too lightly. When he falls in love, he doesn't like to feel that he's signing a treaty. There has to be an escape clause. He never really knows *what* he wants. In fact, he may convince himself that the important thing in life is to know what you *don't* want.

Men born under this sign are frank and outspoken. The truth sometimes hurts, but tact is not the Sagittarian's middle name. On the other hand, if he gives you his word, you can depend on it.

As a friend, he is easygoing, tolerant, broadminded. But once he is your lover, you become a project of his. He will want to help you grow. If he invests time in you and you disappoint him, his attraction will turn to resentment. He is not above petty criticism or silent sulking. He is a perfectionist who demands mental and physical compatibility in the one he loves. But his criticism is also a sign that he feels close to you.

He has a tendency toward secrecy and will keep a relationship hidden even when it isn't really necessary. Moody and easily depressed, he may also suffer from occasional nervousness and even strange delusions. Fortunately, these spells don't last long.

You may be taken aback by his temper tantrums. He likes to do his own thing and does not willingly make concessions. Experience has taught him that he can get almost anything he sets his ambition to.

He is very practical in managing finances, but his weakness is that he will sometimes waste his powers on enterprises not worthy of him. You'll find him generous. He enjoys luxury and gives lavish presents.

He is an excellent raconteur and a charming guest at parties. He prefers small gatherings: too many people under one roof make him uncomfortable. In fact, he would prefer not to be under a roof at all. He enjoys the wide open spaces under a cloudless sky and the stars.

He loves to travel. The constantly shifting scene, the endless new faces, contacts, and experiences are perfectly suited to the Sagittarian temperament. He is the prototype of the man who went to a travel agent and asked for a ticket to anywhere "because I've got friends all over."

He is always looking for facts. His curiosity is insatiable, and he takes great interest in sexual education.

A woman who marries a Sagittarian should bear in mind that this is a man who, whether married or single, remains in his heart a bachelor.

HIS SEX LIFE

You remember the song about the fellow who, when he could not be near the girl he loved, loved the girl he was near? He must have been a Sagittarian. The Sagittarius male flits from woman to woman like a bee, sucking the nectar from each. He can't help himself. He is in love with an idealized, romanticized dream and must pursue that ideal wherever it may beckon.

Sex with him is rarely an intense experience. He enjoys it but doesn't feel the earth move. Who wants to live in the middle of an earthquake? He prefers to wander in a quiet garden of lovely flowers and pluck the bloom that catches his whim.

The excitement for him is in the chase, the fun in the preliminaries. However, if and when he succeeds in luring a girl into the bedroom, she may be disappointed. The symbol for this sign is the Archer drawing his bow, but his arrow doesn't always hit the target—at least, not the first time! He is Speedy Gonzalez about pushing matters to a quick climax. Wham—bam—sorry ma'am is too often the result, and a woman is left hanging like clothes in a closet. (A little Dibucaine ointment can help here.)

On the other hand, the Sagittarian male is never bored by sex. He *loves* to make love. He'll be the first to try a new position, a different setting—you name it and he'll do it! I recently got a letter from a young woman asking whether her Sagittarius mate's fondness for making love three or four times a day was going to ruin his health. I told her to expect nothing less from a man born under the sign of the Archer.

Sagittarius male is most likely to be an office Lothario, having not one but two or three clandestine affairs at one time. However, if the women involved put their heads together, they might discover that, although their lover is impetuous, he certainly makes up for it in one way. Quantity *can* be a substitute for quality!

He likes oral play and anal sex, and often combines the two. Don't be surprised if he pushes a finger into your rectum to try to bring you to orgasm. By all means buy a couple of dildoes—one for you and one for him. He has a very glib tongue (in more ways than one) and can talk you into doing *anything*.

A master of erotic massage—both oral and manual—his fingers act like little spider legs, lightly touching and stimulating erotic areas. His tongue can be a wicked instrument when applied to a woman's erogenous zones—her nipples, the soft flesh inside her thighs, and the genital area.

Those Sagittarius males who master further steps in this craft of love will sometimes take two small plastic balls and during cunnilingus insert the balls into the vagina. The combined action of tongue, lips, and fingers manipulating the balls usually has an explosive effect.

A sexual hang-up to which many Sagittarius males are subject is frictation—satisfaction achieved by rubbing the genitals against some part of the body of a love partner. A Sagittarius male can be brought to orgasm by a partner simply manipulating his penis between the soles of the feet, in the cleft of the buttocks, or within the armpit. One Sagittarius male told me he particularly enjoyed it when his partner rubbed his organ between the underside of the jaw and the neck!

The Sagittarius man has an extreme interest in women's legs. A calf and thigh clad in sheer nylon will turn him on. He even finds intercourse more exciting if the woman wears her stockings.

The ripple of calf and thigh muscles, the curve of an instep, is sheer eroticism to him. If a woman sits with crossed legs, one shoe dangling—hanging only by the toes—he is ready to flip out.

He has a tendency toward other fetishes. While making love, he may ask the woman to wear gloves or shoes—or both. Or he may hold on to a piece of silk or have her panties, preferably ones she's worn recently, pressed to his nose to inhale the aroma. Any criticism will only bring a wisecrack in response or a verbal counterattack. Seldom embarrassment.

He has a strong bias toward bisexuality. If this becomes overt, he will flit equally from a woman lover to a male lover. Neither will hold his chief devotion. This kind of Sagittarius male would like to change the old Hollywood movie formula to read: Boy meets girl—boy leaves girl—boy gets boy.

His affairs are many and varied. He is as amoral as an alley cat. For him, sex is life, and he wants to experience life to the fullest. He would agree with the famous author Herman Melville, who said, "I try everything; I achieve what I can."

FIRST MOVES

They are warm and interesting talkers, so listen actively and ask the right questions. Show an alert, lively mind, and let Sagittarians flaunt their cleverness. If you're a dummy, find another playmate. Sagittarius only likes people who are alert and responsive. They have a fine sense of humor and don't like party poopers or people who can't keep up a clever conversation.

If you like horses or dogs, you have a natural topic in common. Cats too, although they don't rate quite as high since these domesticated felines don't share Sagittarius's love for the outdoors.

For a first date, do something outdoors. Go swimming at a beach (a nude beach if there is one, for Sagittarius will respond to the unconventional and daring), or suggest a picnic in the woods, horseback riding, skiing, or mountain climbing. But be sure you can keep up. Sagittarians are noted for their stamina.

You can suggest overnight or weekend camping trips. You won't offend by making the suggestion. Sagittarius is frank and open about sex, and never takes offense at anything that seems adventurous or unusual.

You might try a rock concert, particularly if it's outdoors. Or get tickets to a musical comedy or ballet—Sagittarius likes both. They enjoy anything with a lot of music and movement on stage.

If there's a party at home, don't invite a large group. Sagittarius prefers the gathering to be small so they can make a real social impact.

Gifts are welcome. Give them something they can wear outdoors—pigskin driving gloves, a wooly cap and muffler. Or something that appeals to their gypsy instincts—a traveling bag or passport case. It doesn't have to be fancy. Price is not a factor—it's the thought that counts.

The thing to remember is that the Sagittarian is always willing to be your friend. It's up to you if you want the relationship to become more than that.

EROGENOUS ZONES

The hips and thighs are the special erotic area for this ninth sign of the zodiac, but for Sagittarius woman so is her hair. Play with it, stroke it, comb it, brush it, tug at it gently. She will purr like a kitten. And if you keep it up long enough, this alone will ignite her slumbering passions.

His vulnerable area is close to the genitalia. Kisses

inside the thigh, or lightly running the tongue from knee to crotch, will delight him. So will delicately fingering his hips. If homosexual, he likes his male lover to rub Vaseline on his inner thighs. Then, holding his legs tightly together, the simple insertion of a penis with its controlled friction on the thighs and gentle nudging of his testes will bring him to orgasm.

For either male or female Sagittarian: Try a rubdown with warm oil. On the hips use circular motions and on the thighs vertical strokes. Run a fingernail very lightly over the rounded areas—it will shoot erotic sensations up the spine.

And don't be surprised if you *never* get to finish the massage.

LAST MOVES

When all the wheels run down and you're looking for a way out, you won't have much trouble. Sagittarius will doubtless feel the same way. This is one affair you can end without too much *sturm und drang.*

You can hurry things to a conclusion by being dictatorial, trying to tell them how to dress, behave, or conduct themselves in public. Criticize their clothes, pets, friends. Be short-tempered. Look on the dark side. Sagittarius is an optimist who believes opportunity waits on every doorstep. Set them straight about that.

If you want to get rid of a Sagittarian woman, become a moody, silent stay-at-home. Insist she change her job or her hairdo. Refuse to drive thirty miles "just to see a movie." When you go out on a date, flirt with other women.

If a male Sagittarian friend is beginning to wear your nerves thin, throw a large party and invite people he considers undesirable. Complain about his dog's messy ways. Start to nag him about the impracticality of his new ideas, new projects, or "wild-eyed" schemes.

At night keep the windows closed so he'll be denied fresh air. Limit your sexual activity to the bedroom at home.

One morning you'll wake to find a note pinned to your pillow announcing that you're now as free as he is.

YOUR SENSUAL GUIDE

SAGITTARIUS and ARIES: Although they are highly compatible, their mutually combustible natures guarantee plenty of fireworks. However, arguments are short-lived. They get a kick out of doing things together in and out of the bedroom, and will have lots of friends. Both enjoy an active recreational and sports life. If sex is good, everything else should be great. That includes either an affair or marriage.

SAGITTARIUS and TAURUS: Taurus wants to dominate, and Sagittarius won't be dominated. In sex, it's probable that Taurus's steady passions will not be requited by Sagittarius's occasional impulsive desires. Taurus's practical, home-loving nature will also be offended by Sagittarius's restless seeking for adventure. Self-discipline is needed for even a short stay; a minor miracle is needed for a long one.

SAGITTARIUS and GEMINI: They are far too restless and rootless for any true compatibility. They quickly develop other interests and drift off to follow them. Both are fun loving and enjoy each other's company for a time, but Gemini will turn critical and Sagittarius will be driven via the short route to distraction. Nearly hopeless, but on rare occasions it can be exciting.

* * *

SAGITTARIUS and CANCER: These two are at opposite ends of the zodiac. Cancer needs security and stability, while Sagittarius wants to be free to venture. Cancer is too sensitive to put up with outspoken Sagittarius. There might be a workable sexual harmony, but Sagittarius soon feels the iron bars of the cage forming and flies away. They might be better friends than lovers. Poor vibes for the long haul.

SAGITTARIUS and LEO: This relationship offers great openness and freedom. Leo holds the passion key that can unlock Sagittarius. They should be exciting bed companions. Both also respect each other and enjoy each other's company. They share a love for adventure, and cope lightheartedly with difficulties. A fine affair, and this could be a mating made in heaven.

SAGITTARIUS and VIRGO: Their relationship will deteriorate. Sagittarius's happy-go-lucky approach drives Virgo crazy. Sexually they strike occasional sparks, but that still leaves 23½ hours out of the day. Bookish, quiet Virgo, inclined toward a simple life and the passions of the mind, doesn't have much in common with reckless, impulsive, outdoor-loving Sagittarius. In turn, Sagittarius finds Virgo B-O-R-I-N-G. Forget it.

SAGITTARIUS and LIBRA: Libra's tolerance is just what Sagittarius needs. Libra will watch with fond amusement the devil-may-care antics of Sagittarius. Both are sexually responsive, and considerate Libra will bring out the best in this partner. They will enjoy each other, find little reason to quarrel, and will have many friends and outside-the-home interests. Good vibes here both for the short and long term.

SAGITTARIUS and SCORPIO: Sagittarius thwarts Scorpio's passionate nature. Trouble lurks if Sagittarius follows a natural inclination toward freedom and independence, for Scorpio's need is for a loyal mate who can be depended on. Sagittarius has a quick temper that soon cools; Scorpio's anger broods forever until it erupts like a volcano. Physically they may be compatible for a time, but marriage won't be a many-splendored thing.

SAGITTARIUS and SAGITTARIUS: An exciting but chaotic combination. There is always something cooking, but whose fat is in the fire? The general unpredictability of their lifestyles makes a combination that brings out the worst in both. Their restless, independent natures will sooner or later seek freedom—from each other. They are ships that pass in the night; they won't make port together on a long voyage.

SAGITTARIUS and CAPRICORN: Capricorn's cautious, plotting nature is appalled by the impulsive carelessness of Sagittarius. Capricorn's demands prove irksome, and Sagittarius's frank, outspoken reaction offends Capricorn. Money also presents a problem—Capricorn is thrifty, and Sagittarius is a free spender who wants everything money can buy. A rising tide of discontent swamps these two.

SAGITTARIUS and AQUARIUS: Level-headed Aquarius can keep this relationship on an even keel. They share a love for adventure and for getting involved in outside affairs. Sex will be innovative, whether in the bedroom or on a bed of pine needles in a forest. Neither is jealous, and neither will try to dominate the other. They should be fun-loving, imaginative lovers whose relationship will deepen in marriage.

SAGITTARIUS and PISCES: Neither provides the reliability that the other requires. There are moments of passion but the sword of Damocles hangs on a frayed thread over this couple. Sagittarius feels hemmed in by Pisces's timidity, and its energy and optimism slowly sink into a swamp of depression. A most difficult romance and a virtually impossible marriage.

CAPRICORN

December 22–January 19

THE FEMALE

Her passions are incurably orderly. She would schedule a gang rape.

No matter what you've heard, Capricorn women *are* passionate. What she needs is immoral courage. You may have to persuade her to let her emotions hang out.

Until she gets over her cautious approach to love, she won't know real fulfillment. To put it another way, when she is too cautious, she ends up having caution itself to be cautious about. Her aloofness will yield as soon as she becomes more sure of herself—and of you. She loves to be loved.

Her gaze is never fixed on the stars; she is too well grounded in earth. And she isn't going to be impulsive about sex. She's lusty enough for any man, but she's got herself well under control.

She's all there for a man to admire, court, pursue—and never completely possess. She knows what you want, but you will never be quite sure what she is thinking. Many men find her hard to figure out. Others find her reserve and aloofness tantalizing, perhaps because they know it's a cover for extremely powerful emotions. But her constant turning on and turning off can finally make any lover dizzy.

And yet . . .

When all the flashy, scintillating, brilliant, and available women have passed into memory, *she* will remain. She's the one whose telephone number you never forget. And unless you're made of sterner stuff than most men, you won't be able to resist dialing her number.

The truth is, she's afraid of falling in love because she wants to be sure it's the real thing. Basically, she needs to feel secure and protected.

Once committed to a lover, she isn't likely to withdraw her affections. She is an all-or-nothing woman. She is extremely loyal.

But she must be loved and wanted in return. That's why she must be aloof and cautious at first; she's trying to size up the possibilities and risks before committing herself. Her emotional guard is up. Unfortunately, she doesn't always know when to let it down. However, the man who really captures and proves worthy of her affections will find an eagerly passionate love partner—a woman who will do anything for her lover.

When she makes a mistake in choosing a mate, it's usually a big one. Many times, however, she is able to transform a mistake into an asset. She has the patience, the stamina, the persistence to do it. In a contest of wills, she is a most formidable antagonist. If you really try to hurt her, beware. She won't forget or forgive. With her, revenge knows no statute of limitations.

She will always be a separate, independent person who insists on living her own life. During an affair, she may insist on the right to go out where, when, and with whom she pleases. In marriage she may demand her own car, her own bank account. If she has a job, she may continue to use her own name at work. She'll find some way to tell you, "'I've Got To Be Me.'"

But she is definitely all woman and knows the value of enhancing beauty. She has an instinct for neatness and cleanliness, tends to be thorough and careful in applying makeup, and has very feminine tastes in dress and accessories. Other women often come to her for advice on how to dress to attract men.

She is calculating. She will attempt to dominate a man and use him to advance her own designs. Weak men are drawn to the Capricorn female. She is flattered by their attention but will not let them become a burden.

Formal and stand-offish in her youth, as she gets older she becomes more sure of herself. She will usually marry late in life after having had many alliances. But she is no man's sexual plaything. She is far too shrewd for that. Her passions run deep and she can become physically or emotionally ill without love, but she will never settle for a mere lover as her lifetime mate. She wants someone to satisfy *all* her needs.

She must be constantly busy to be happy and often becomes involved with charities or causes. She takes life quite seriously and has an inner conviction of her ability to attain high goals. The trouble is that she is never sure when she gets there. There is always some further goal to reach, some new ambition for which she must gird herself. She is never completely satisfied.

She respects people who are successful and is willing to accept instruction from them. She admires and obeys authority. There is an easy way to get around her unfortunate tendency to be snobbish: Pay her compliments. She *loves* to be complimented. Once she feels confident that she is accepted and admired, she becomes much more human.

Quiet, unflamboyant, competent—she does not always get her just due. Others with less talent tend to push her aside. But only for a time. In the end, she will prevail despite setbacks, discouragements, disappointments, or delays.

That's how she is.

HER SEX LIFE

She is quick tinder.

Sometimes you can ignite her fire with just a gesture, a caress. And it won't be a smoldering brush fire but a roaring conflagration.

Don't be offended if she prefers twin beds. That's only because she wants privacy. When she's in the mood for love, and she is often, you won't mind the commuting.

She doesn't need much foreplay, for she accelerates from zero to wow! in nothing flat. She likes to take the lead in lovemaking. She may start the proceedings in a shower stall or a bathtub. Then talcumed, perfumed, or oiled, she is ready to move on to the next room and the next act. Don't try to surprise her. She always likes to know what's next on the program.

Because of her great sexual endurance, she also expects a lover to keep up. She's not interested in exotic variation, only in staying power. Far-out experimentation doesn't start the colored pinwheels going for her. After all, she gets great results with the conventional varieties of lovemaking. She can't see why it's necessary to knock yourself out with the acrobatics of position forty-one when the missionary position leads by a more direct route to equal transports of delight. As a famous baseball manager said, "If you've got a fastball and a curve, who needs a slider and a spitter?"

However, since she likes to dominate in the act of lovemaking, she is especially pleased by the variant position in which she is astride the male. There, she has control of the situation. Let him suck on her breasts or knead them, and she will manipulate his penis with her fingers and vagina. What's important is that she sets a rhythm to please herself. When he's ready to go, so is she.

Once into the rhythm, she goes all the way to crescendo. She's a scratcher and a screamer. Lovemaking becomes a wild contest with orgasm as the prize. You can depend on it: She will get there. More than once.

She likes prolonged lovemaking and has an unusual capacity for making love often. One satisfying solution: the vibrafinger, a vibrating machine with a rubber reproduction of a human finger at one end. When men give out, vibrators can be a woman's best friend.

She enjoys cunnilingus but will perform fellatio only when the resulting erection is used to *her* satisfaction. She is not interested in a one-sided affair where she is left out at the critical moment.

Animal skins strewn about the floor or on the bed will please her. She finds the sensation of short animal hairs shifting, tingling, and moving under skin erotically stimulating.

One tip: The pad of your big toe on her clitoris or vulva will drive her wild. A touch there can start her engine racing. You might even try using that big toe in her armpit—many Capricorn females dig the armpit as a source of sexual pleasure.

Often calculating in her sexual drives, her need to be satisfied approaches nymphomania. When she reaches her climax, she wants to feel the earth move. That's all she cares about.

Beware: She's a biter. Sometimes this is erotic, but when the lovebite occurs immediately before or during orgasm she isn't aware of how deep and hard she's going into flesh. The jaws tend to lock during orgasm, so she may inadvertently become cannibalistic. *That* kind of pain won't turn anyone on.

Other hang-ups also tend to the sadistic. A spanking, either with palm or wooden paddle, applied with vigor to the buttocks before the sex act will bring her to a fever pitch. Don't make the mistake of thinking *she's* the one to get spanked. It's dealing out punishment to a male partner that brings her passions to the proper level of anticipatory excitement. If *he* likes it though, who's to complain?

She also enjoys pushing a vibrator into a man's anus. It's one of her favorite sexual tricks because it serves a double purpose: His erection becomes more rigid and the vibrator causes him to buck and rear like a bronco, thereby enhancing her pleasurable sensation.

The Capricorn woman may appear cold, but that is only protective armor. Once she sheds that armor, you can unleash a load of surprises from this lovely Pandora's box!

THE MALE

When you say goodnight and start to close the door, his foot will be in the way. He won't take no for an answer. A turndown is not a turnoff. He will try again and again until he wears down resistance. Of course, there are ways of saying no that can sound like yes—or at least maybe. But why say no?

Capricorn is the sign of the Goat, and he brings to lovemaking all the lustful gusto of that four-footed animal. Love is as necessary to him as eating or sleeping.

Probably you began to suspect during your first date that this is an earthy, lusty male—the kind who expects a woman to comply with his wishes. He believes that inside every virtuous woman there is a wanton trying to get out. He also places greater value on the sex act than on the woman involved. You can bet that Capricorn men make up a sizable segment of male chauvinist pigs.

The Capricorn male is not as innately cruel as Scorpio, but his strong sexuality does make him unscrupulous. He cheerfully takes advantage of inexperience or naiveté, and is attracted to partners much younger than himself.

He is passionate, strongly sensual, and hates to be refused anything. He won't put up with any coy teasing from a woman. He resents wasting his time. However, he *will* understand if you have well-reasoned objections to leaping into bed with him; he can be patient. An honest statement of how you feel will be enough—if that is how you really feel. Don't try to put on an act. He not only won't like it, he'll see through it.

What he basically needs is to be assured that you like him. He demands much because he wants you to commit yourself. If you give his ego enough encouragement, make it clear how much you enjoy his company, he'll be tied to your kite strings for as long as you want him. He's faithful. He doesn't understand why so many men feel the need to stray. If you have one good woman, how many do you need? Capricorn is content to be yours alone.

He prefers to stay at home rather than gad about to parties and entertainments. That doesn't mean your domestic life will be dull. Sexy Capricorn can't get enough of bedroom activity—and the older he gets, the better he gets. His interest in the physical side of love never wanes. When other men are resigned to their rocking chairs, aging Capricorn—or should I call him Old Goat?—will still be trying to lure women into the bedroom. And his technique only improves with age!

Though he needs a satisfying sexual relationship, that alone is not enough. A woman must fulfill him in other areas. He expects you to be a great hostess, a working partner, a loyal friend. He needs a sense that you two are linked by a romantic destiny. But he won't agonize about it. As a Capricorn male once told me, "Once you accept the fact that happiness is not all it's cracked up to be, you can be perfectly happy." He is money-oriented. He is also careful, cautious, calculating, and uncompromising. He will always discharge what he considers his duty. In a conflict of wills, don't look for a reasonable compromise. Even if he appears to bargain, he will just be stalling for time.

You never know what he's up to. He manages to conceal his thoughts behind a moody and introspective mask. One thing you *can* be sure of—deep within his quiet surface secret fires are burning.

His progress toward a goal is as relentless and deliberate as a lava flow. He is a firm believer in singleness of purpose. He knows that all the talent in the world is useless without the ability to work. This is the key to his success in either love or business.

A born manager, he will usually climb to the top in whatever field he chooses. He is practical, determined, and ambitious. Those who do him favors along the way will always be rewarded handsomely. If misfortune should strike, he is tough and resilient and will bounce back.

It is true that Capricorn males are more likely to marry for money than those of other signs. Their practical natures see no reason why love cannot follow self-interest. Isn't it just as easy to fall for a rich woman as a poor one? There is nothing more romantic about making love in a garret than in an expensive condominium. Nor does having to skip a meal occasionally do much to enhance the sexual appetite.

Fundamentally, however, he is a sensualist. He seeks the heights of love through sheer physical passion. In an emotional relationship, he demands much and gives as little as possible of himself. He won't go out of his way to please or to be charming. As far as he's concerned, the least important way to achieve success in love is to be lovable.

With his attitude toward women and with his skills in money management, it's little wonder that so many Capricorn males become pimps, skin-flick producers, or peddlers of pornography.

HIS SEX LIFE

Sex evokes the best he can offer. He believes, and will convince you, that a person only really understands what love is if he or she understands physical passion. Coitus is not an impulsive act for him. He schedules his sexual activity as he schedules his entire life. In love, as in everything else, he is a planner and a schemer.

He prefers a woman to know what he enjoys and not compel him to make the first move or exert himself too much. After all, you can't build a bridge just on one side. A woman must learn the little tricks that arouse him and arrange surprises of the kind he will enjoy. And whenever he desires her, he expects her to be ready, willing, and enthusiastic.

He is proud of his sexual prowess and his ability to satisfy a woman by making that last bit of effort. He has the stamina of a marathon runner. He'll keep it up right to your finish line.

Among Capricorns you find the kind of man who will go almost to the point of orgasm, withdraw, allow the woman to fellate him, and still hold off until she is ready to scream. Sex is a ritual, an unwinding of pressures and tensions he does not acknowledge but which he is only able to exorcize in this particular way.

If a woman tries to outlast him by interrupting their lovemaking to change to a new position, or go into the bathroom for more Koromex cream, it won't bother him. He will simply masturbate to keep his erection until she returns.

Lovemaking, he believes, should take place in comfort, on a well-upholstered bed or on a thick bearskin rug before a fire. And it should be accompanied by dim lights, soft music, and rare liquor.

However, don't tell him what to do or how to it.

Relax. He will take pride in being able to satisfy you. He senses what you like and will improve upon it. Let him know you enjoy making love with him. That will encourage him to do even better.

A favorite technique of his is the sexual waltz: a slow striptease while dancing together. The sensuous movements excite him. When you're both naked, he may bring you to bed or take you while you're dancing and continue in slow rhythm locked in each other's arms. If you're much shorter than he, he'll pick you up in his arms while you wrap your legs around his waist, your arms about his neck—and let the music play, *maestro*.

Another erotic tip that delights a Capricorn male by its unexpectedness: The woman inserts the nipple of her breast into the opening of his penis. He'll love it and love you for doing it.

A very big turn-on for Capricorn male is gagging his sexual partner. The sight of a naked woman well-gagged by a cloth (*never* adhesive tape—it hurts to peel off) rouses that never-too-latent male desire to commit rape on a helpless woman.

Warning: Play this game at your own risk. It often leads to simulated rape. He can get rough and will hurt a woman. He'll rip off your clothes, squeeze your breasts painfully, pin you down so you can't resist. The more effort you make to avoid him, the more he'll be stimulated.

Some women enjoy it.

But this sort of simulated rape can lead to more extreme forms of sadism, such as bondage games. He'll stake out a woman on a bed, her wrists and ankles bound, while he subjects her to varied forms of sexual abuse. For Capricorns with hang-ups, a strong kinship exists between sexual emotion and cruelty.

A youthful insecurity regarding girls inclines him toward masturbation, even to mutual masturbation with homosexuals. He may carry such habits into adulthood. During many years of studying Capricorns, I have found them particularly subject to the kind of sexual aberration known as natelism, in which the penis is rested in the cleavage of fleshy buttocks and moved at different rhythms until orgasm. Some refine this action by pausing to kiss and fondle the buttocks.

Since he prides himself on his staying power, he will go to great lengths to extend it. A favorite way is the so-called penis ring made of leather or an elaborate cord laced with gold string. Once he achieves an erection, he places the ring at the base of the penis, enabling him to hold his erection for long periods. Sometimes he wears a penis ring with prongs that will *really* stimulate her.

Capricorns lend themselves easily to certain kinds of perversions and sadism. Many prefer to reach a climax by penetrating the woman through the anus. One Capricorn male I know insists on the woman taking an enema and then having intercourse while her bowels remain swollen. The added pressure on her during the sex act adds to his sexual pleasure.

The key to understanding Capricorn's hang-ups is to realize that his total involvement with *himself* usually means he excludes any real consideration for his sexual partner.

If he meets with resistance, he is likely to use force.

FIRST MOVES

Capricorns are work-oriented and ambitious. You may find them in adult classes at the local university or browsing through the self-help bookshelf at the library. Being great do-gooders, they are usually embroiled in the service of various causes and organizations. An excellent way to get to know them is to become involved in such organizations and to work side by side with them.

However, they are shrewd and can readily discern when a person is sincere or merely acting out of an ulterior motive. They also know the difference between a sincere compliment and a smooth line. Don't write too-flowery letters or make overly impassioned protestations of love. That will succeed in getting you labeled as a "phony."

Capricorns are interested in the arts and theater and are drawn to people who are intellectually stimulating. Discuss books, painting, music, politics—but it's well to bone up beforehand so you'll have something interesting to say. Never adopt as your own an opinion or attitude that you really don't subscribe to. Capricorn is quick to spot a pretender. On the other hand, Capricorn loves to play the role of professor. If you think Winslow Homer is a third baseman for the Cleveland Indians, confess your ignorance—and let Capricorn teach you.

At a social gathering, Capricorn is usually in the background taking it all in. He probably isn't the most stimulating date you've ever known. The wit isn't going to sparkle like champagne, and if you whip up a frothy conversation it's likely to lie there like soggy pudding. He is more likely to open up when you discuss serious topics—the news of the world and, especially, finances. He keeps up with what is going on and expects that you do. If so, you won't have any trouble keeping his attention and, in the end, capturing his interest.

They are very aware of money values and try to collect things that have lasting value. You can please her (naturally!) with an expensive diamond ring, but she will also be happy with a much less costly but lovely antique ring that will increase in value as years go by.

The male Capricorn will be grateful for a set of

distinctive cufflinks, a rare book, or an original painting—especially if the artist shows promise. Someday, it may be a masterpiece!

One tip: Capricorns are fond of their families. If you're trying to impress her by buying first-night tickets to a show, invest your money instead in *three* tickets later in the week—and take her mother along. You'll be in like Flynn, guaranteed.

They like to dine well and in classy surroundings. If you're going to ply her with champagne, get a good brand. If you're making dinner at home, don't break out the peanut butter and jelly. Plan a meal that will look as good as it tastes. Candlelight and a really good wine will enhance the occasion. Male Capricorn is impressed by a woman who knows her way around a kitchen. And he loves being catered to.

The final setting for love should be a place that *looks* elegantly furnished and luxurious—even if it isn't really. Capricorns don't like anything cheap or squalid. For them it's got to be first class all the way!

EROGENOUS ZONES

Capricorn male likes a woman to slide her nipples slowly over his face, mouth, chest, stomach, and groin. It can drive him out of his mind.

Female Capricorn's passion will attain hurricane force if her mate kisses her on the navel or behind her knees. The skin around the navel is particularly sensitive in women born under this sign. And the skin at the back of her knee reacts to sensory stimuli much as the inside of the upper thigh does in other women.

Either male or female Capricorn will react to a massage that starts with the lower back and gently strokes upward along either side of the spine, then uses the tongue in slow short circles around the spinal vertebra.

In my experience as a consultant, I've discovered an unusual percentage of Capricorns who claim to get a thrill out of axilism. This is a form of frictation in which the armpit is used as a source of sexual pleasure.

You take it from there.

LAST MOVES

When Capricorn has had enough, he or she will walk out. No loud words, quarrels, or physical violence. Capricorn just goes.

Getting him or her to that point isn't difficult.

Make fun of their inability to sparkle. Tell her she has a mind like a clogged sink. Ask the male Capricorn if his ability to be boring was inherited.

They cannot stand being teased. Although they enjoy jokes, they cannot tolerate being the butt of them. Practical jokes are a particular anathema. That also applies to scatological jokes. Capricorn males and females share a loathing for humor of the "bathroom" variety.

Criticize endlessly. They abhor any kind of criticism.

Capricorn women have an especially deep love and respect for their immediate family. Insult her mother, sneer at her father, snub the kid brother.

Spend money on trivia.

Stage a lot of jealous scenes. Capricorns resent any show of possessiveness that intrudes on their highly developed sense of privacy.

Refuse to keep any sort of a schedule or program. Eat only when you're hungry, sleep only when you're tired, and make love only if the spirit moves you, no matter where you happen to be or what you happen to be doing.

Try to make them live in a social whirl. Even in the best of all possible social whirls, they're miserable.

Drink so much that you have trouble putting your eyeballs back into their sockets and you continually break out into ribald song.

There's your Capricorn Goat bounding away—never to be seen again.

YOUR SENSUAL GUIDE

CAPRICORN and ARIES: Both are strong-willed, aggressive, and won't be bossed. If you think that's a set-up for combat rather than romance, you're probably right. While they may be compatible in bed, there will be arguments about money, friends, who will make decisions, and career. Throw in a little jealousy just to keep the cauldron bubbling. An affair might work. Marriage is much less promising.

CAPRICORN and TAURUS: Both would rather stay home than gad about, both value money, both think security is all important. Taurus has patience and Capricorn is willing to work toward a common goal of mutual enjoyment. Sexually this couple can dream the impossible dream—and make it come true. Capricorn's ambition also meshes well with Taurus's determination. Fine vibes all around.

CAPRICORN and GEMINI: Distinctly different sexual personalities. Gemini is impulsive, flirtatious, and excitable. Capricorn is slow, faithful, and cautious. Any initial attraction is the fabled one of opposites and can't endure. Ambitious, materialistic Capricorn will not long tolerate Gemini's capricious, indecisive ways. Love can't conquer all.

CAPRICORN and CANCER: Cancer is a little shy sexually, but Capricorn is willing to take the lead. More demonstrativeness from both would help in the preliminaries.

Any rapport they establish in the bedroom will be sorely needed to see them past other obstacles. They are zodiac opposites with all that implies. Capricorn will become too demanding and domineering for sensitive Cancer. An affair is just a matter of time.

CAPRICORN and LEO: Leo thinks Capricorn is stingy with affection, doling it out like pennies. Capricorn is also too unimaginative a partner for Leo, who likes more fire between the sheets. They don't suit each other well physically, and they are both independent and dominant signs who try to rule outside the bedroom. In an affair these differences may be ignored; in a marriage it just isn't likely.

CAPRICORN and VIRGO: Capricorn's practicality and Virgo's neatness go very well together. Sexual fireworks may start to sputter soon after the affair begins, but other traits work together so harmoniously that perhaps these two won't care. And if they don't, who else should? Both are dependable, conservative, understanding—and those are good auguries for a union that will last even if it doesn't sizzle.

CAPRICORN and LIBRA: Libra's charm and sexual magnetism attract Capricorn at first, but when the bloom is off the rose Capricorn finds Libra too self-centered and unresponsive to its physical needs. Unable to express its feelings, Capricorn looks for other lovers. Thorny going in an affair. Marriage won't work unless there is financial gain in the alliance to satisfy Capricorn.

CAPRICORN and SCORPIO: Sex between these two is gratifying. Scorpio is more imaginative and Capricorn more methodical, but they are quite compatible in this area and success in the bedroom opens up other areas of affection. Both are strong-willed, but Scorpio tends to dominate. Capricorn understands that Scorpio's possessiveness is really a symptom of love. A passionate affair, and a successful marriage.

CAPRICORN and SAGITTARIUS: Capricorn likes to have sex in a comfortable setting; Sagittarius will screw on a freshly dug grave. Capricorn wants to stay at home; Sagittarius is a rover. Capricorn is cautious and conservative and worried about security, and Sagittarius is a gambler. Extravagant and irresponsible, Sagittarius will annoy thrifty, duty-conscious Capricorn. Not a blissful affair, and an unhappy marriage.

CAPRICORN and CAPRICORN: Their romantic life quickly settles into a rut. It can only be successful if both are willing to accept less than they originally hoped for. Neither will experiment or in any way try to enlarge their horizons. The bedroom becomes a suburb of Dullsville. On the other hand, both work hard, are frugal, and serious-minded. An affair or a marriage may not be much fun, but they might satisfy each other.

CAPRICORN and AQUARIUS: A race to decide how quickly romance can turn into friendship. On close intimacy, Aquarius is a little too much for Capricorn to handle. Aquarius prefers unorthodox sex and Capricorn the conventional ways. Freedom-loving, unconventional Aquarius can't stay in love with staid, practical Capricorn. A tolerable affair; a marriage really requires work.

CAPRICORN and PISCES: Pisces will try to con Capricorn, because that's the way Pisces is—but Capricorn can handle that and in bed will take control. Pisces is soon eager to follow. Pisces is also loving and sincere enough to keep Capricorn happy and secure. These very different people supply each other's emotional needs. Good auguries for an affair or a more lasting relationship.

AQUARIUS

January 20–February 18

THE FEMALE

She resents being treated as a sex object. Her high standards are not easily compromised, and she insists that a lover show her a proper respect.

She doesn't like to be rushed. If you're on a first date, don't expect to end up in her bed, because you won't. She doesn't consider a second date the equivalent of a prolonged courtship either. She's not a prude, but you have to convince her that you don't regard her as simply a one-night stand.

The Aquarius woman is sensitive and possesses a very strong intellect. She lives essentially in her mind.

Friends stimulate her. She likes parties and people, excels in socializing, and is always ready to accept a last-minute invitation from someone she likes. Basically honest and open, she is a very poor liar because she doesn't want to be untruthful. When she likes someone, she has a tendency to bare her soul, too often not wisely.

Aquarius female gets involved in the lives of others. She is truly the Waterbearer, giving of herself to others. Sometimes, she'll offer advice that is neither needed nor wanted.

She doesn't mind doing a man's work. She'll take a job as an auto mechanic, road builder, or bricklayer if necessary—but you'll find her most often as an executive on a high corporate level.

What interests her is a challenge. She welcomes any new opportunity, accepts any new responsibility, because she feels certain that she will prove equal to whatever is asked of her. Because she is bright, willing to try anything, and understands the motivations of people, she will usually succeed. She is at her best in working with others, a quality for which John D.

Rockefeller once said he would pay more than for any other.

A true humanitarian, she is very much concerned with the problems of the world she lives in. Look for her in the forefront of any battle for social justice and you'll find her in the underdog's corner. Her native empathy and compassion make her very sensitive to the suffering of others. Yet she is not an obvious do-gooder, seeking appreciation and love in return for her effort. She becomes so engrossed in the work itself that she almost loses sight of the people she is working for. Even when she cares the most, this quality of impersonality, of aloofness, will be apparent.

She is, above all, an individual who has the courage of her convictions and will pursue them to the finish. If a project ends in failure she won't be depressed, for she knows that you can learn as much from a failure as from a success. A worthy attempt that fails is much more attractive to her than some minor success, for it is an invitation to reach out and try again.

Although she is charming, entertaining, and imaginative, she can be stubborn. For example, many Aquarius women are strong believers in the occult, and you will find it useless to try to change their minds. If they are sure they *know* something, they are not going to be swayed by argument or even by "facts." They are aware that "facts" are often proved wrong by those who pioneer in realms which others fear. When she makes up her mind, only *she* can change it. (And she often does, sometimes unexpectedly.)

Because of her deep need for love and companionship, she finds the opposite sex extremely attractive. But she's looking for the perfect companion and has great difficulty making up her mind. It isn't surprising that she tends to marry late in life, and when she does her choice often surprises her conventional friends. (In fact, her attitudes about controversial subjects always shock conservative friends.) She wants a man who'll really make her feel like a woman, and race, color, and creed don't matter.

She loves beautiful things, including all parts of the human body. You'd better not forget to compliment her on how great she looks in the buff. This woman needs to be appreciated.

She's very neat. When you've just had a tumble between the sheets and are feeling rumpled and lazy, she may want to get up so she can make the bed.

She can be intense, nervous and, when frustrated, something of a nag. Another fault is that she spends too much and is extravagant about personal comforts. Of course she doesn't agree that's a fault. She considers people who devote their lives to the pursuit of money as shallow or a little crazy. The only possible use for money is what it can buy. And she'll go to any lengths to get what she wants.

HER SEX LIFE

She is a slow starter. Animal drives are not all-important to her. She prefers to idealize love, encompass it with tenderness. Love is a Mozart symphony, not the Rolling Stones. Don't come to her bed looking for uncontrolled abandon.

But once you have her aroused, anything goes! She is extremely imaginative and creative, and takes a lively interest in trying new ways of enjoyment. There's nothing in any sex manual she won't try, and she'll probably come up with an interesting variation on their variation.

She believes anything is worthwhile that will increase the pleasure of her lover. I know one inventive Aquarius female who pushed a string of small rubber beads into her lover's anus. As she pulled them out one at a time during the height of lovemaking, it gave him orgasm after orgasm. In the bedroom you only have to suggest something; she will happily oblige.

She loves to run her fingertips lightly over your body hair, all the way from ankles to the groin. Sometimes she varies the intensity of the stroke, from feather-light to a slight rake with the fingernails. Then she'll reach behind, take your buttocks in each hand, and begin to move them in delightfully maddening circles. Often she combines this with oral action up front—and that's when any man starts thinking it's love, l-o-v-e, L-O-V-E.

Her warmth and understanding are particularly effective with men who are inhibited or psychologically impotent. Because she is especially sympathetic to the sexually deprived male, she is fair game for the "dirty old man." I knew an Aquarius woman who, because heat helped her older lover maintain his erection, always made love with him in a sauna—perspiring all the while! Actually, one of Aquarius's difficulties in life is that, in her desire to please, she frequently puts the needs of others ahead of her own. When she is disappointed in love, she turns readily to masturbation for relief.

Aquarius is victimized by husbands whose wives don't understand them. She's a pushover for anyone who plays on her sympathies, but for her to really care about a man she must like his mind as well as his body. Fortunately, she is quite aware that a man's mind is his most erotic organ. Whispering exactly what she intends to do to him can be as stimulating as looking at a nude centerfold in *Penthouse*.

She is fond of head to foot coupling. As she sucks her lover's toe, she may tickle the sole of his foot with a feather. When she licks his testicles, she will massage his penis in the warmth of the hollow of her neck. She *always* has ideas of her own.

Nothing is too far out or taboo. Her need to please includes doing anything her lover's libido desires. If chicken blood liberally sprinkled on her navel and crotch turns him on, she will accept it without a protest. In anal intercourse she will welcome anything from saliva to a lubricant spiked with vitamin E. Oral sex can include ejecting semen into her face and hair. If her lover likes it, it can't be wrong!

One of her more popular variations is the "wink job." She puts on long artificial eyelashes and then runs her blinking eyelids up and down the shaft of the penis until the man reaches orgasm.

Her sympathies, especially for "dirty old men," will in extreme cases lead to incest. If she has a widowed father, she will comfort him with everything from a well-cooked meal to satisfying him in bed. Of course, she will do the same for a brother who is neglected. In her desire to help, she sees no reason to exclude the gift of her body.

The same "understanding" is extended to women. Aquarius will drift into a lesbian affair simply because she can't stand seeing a friend unhappy because of lack of sex.

THE MALE

The first contact has to be made through the mind. He has to respect you as a person before he can be turned on to your charms. Once he is intrigued on an intellectual level, he can be reached on the physical plane. But he cannot attain sexual fulfillment without a previous mind-to-mind contact.

Aquarius is definitely not a loner. He is generous, open, sincerely interested in other people. In fact, he is only happy when involved in the lives of others. He has many friends, and will cheerfully stay up half the night discussing a friend's problems. He is always searching for an answer, searching for the truth. His nature is analytical. The best way to capture his interest is to present him with a problem of yours. He is always curious, inventive, eager to help.

Shy and passive, he usually waits for the female to make the first move. On your first date you may have to take the initiative. That doesn't mean he's indifferent. For him passion has to be intertwined with friendship, and friendship is not something that happens overnight.

His tendency is to run on a low voltage. That also applies in business affairs. He's creative but not a hard worker. You may have to juice him up from time to time but this must be done with tact, for Aquarius resists domination. He resents having to make explanations to you or anyone, and a small misunderstanding can drive him into a shell. Outwardly cool, he is highly emotional.

Don't ask him to conform. He can't. His only way of dealing with tradition is to break it. That's the way progress happens, in his opinion. As one fellow born under this sign informed me, "You can travel around the world and you won't find any statues put up to people who were in favor of the status quo. Nobody builds statues to conservatives."

It's an absolute waste of time to try to pin him down. He must be free and independent. Naturally he loves to travel. A not-so-happy consequence of his independence is that, despite many companions, he often cannot develop a really profound friendship. He shuns the ties that bind, even when they are the bonds of friendship.

In company he appears eager to please and delighted to meet people, but most people sooner or later observe that there has been little real contact. Aquarius male slips away from you like quicksilver in the hand. He becomes bored and soon turns his attention to other people, other pursuits.

Confronted with a challenge, he wants to grapple directly with it. This is true of him in sports as well as in business. He hates to "warm up" and would far rather plunge directly into the contest. In television, Aquarius actors are notorious for their ability to memorize scripts quickly and to "come up" for a role without rehearsal. They are natural performers and orators and have an unusual ability to convince others.

In romance, Aquarius male responds to the subtle approach and is capable of the tenderest emotions. He is highly imaginative sexually—a frigid woman won't remain frigid long with him for a lover!

Unfortunately, he often loses himself in dreaming rather than doing and wastes his sex energies in erotic fantasies and masturbation.

He is restless, always looking for the perfect mate. He may fall in love easily but hesitates to marry. If you finally get him on the hook, you'll find he's a great catch. He is perceptive, kind, expressive, vivacious, and a good judge of character. He really likes people, and people really like him. Though he may have appeared cool on the surface, he smolders with masculine magnetism.

What's more, though he's always attracted to the new and unusual (Uranus, his ruler, is the planet of the unexpected), he's basically faithful. If he's occasionally flirtatious, that's because he's so curious about the unknown. Keep a loose rein and he'll come home again.

He can be a lot of fun—and very stimulating—for the right woman.

HIS SEX LIFE

He is interested in a woman as an individual—not as a sex object. Many women think it wonderful to have a man as interested in their minds as in their bodies.

His approach will be slow and considerate. He prefers to enjoy the varieties of foreplay for a while before getting right down to the whiskers. This contrasts with his reluctance to "warm up" in other activities, but the explanation is simple. Foreplay is a very important part of "the game" to him.

In fact, his patient approach might qualify him as a real artist of lovemaking, except for his unfortunate tendency to stay at the preliminaries too long. You may have to urge him along. He can become so turned on to the delights of foreplay that he'll actually overlook orgasm! As a consultant I'm always amazed at the number of women who tell me that their Aquarius lovers prolong matters to a point where they are brought to orgasm without real penetration. The answer is not that the men lack the capacity—they just don't make up their minds!

Once his engine is revved up, however, he is a free and inventive lover with amazing persistence. He'll see you through to a satisfying climax. In fact, you have about as much chance to divert him as to change a river from its course.

A woman who knows what she wants can make him do anything. It's all in the approach. One woman with an Aquarius lover came to me with this problem: He wouldn't perform cunnilingus. I told her to try a liberal coating of honey on her vagina. It worked (Aquarius being very oral). But also being Aquarius, since then he's insisted on a different flavor each time—everything from raspberry jam to oil of jasmine!

He'll try the newest and most exotic erotica. Skin thimbles are made to order for Aquarius. These are finger gloves, hardly longer than a conventional thimble, each of which is covered with a different kind of fur or bristle or even a tuft of tiny needle-like projections of a pliable material. The thimbles are used to massage sexually sensitive parts of the body.

Love is a playground for the Aquarius male, and he seldom plays a scene the same way. He is a true sex "scientist" and avidly reads all the books he can find on the subject. He is the type who will go through the *Kama Sutra* and try all the positions at least once. If the woman suggests she'd like a *ménage à trois* one night, he'll happily join in. And he'll make sure everyone reaches climax twice—once orally and once genitally. Next week he'll bring along *two* friends and make it a four-way scene!

Quickly bored with the same lovemaking position, he likes the complicated variations—such as holding the woman's legs in a wheelbarrow position while she rests her head on the floor. Sometimes his experimentation raises a partner to new heights of ecstasy, and at other times leaves her uncomfortable, unsatisfied, and in pain. Unfortunately, you can't put him off by telling him anything he does is immoral or abnormal. Aquarius is the most tolerant, broad-minded sign in the zodiac, so nothing human is alien to him.

One of his favorite toys is the Japanese box. The box has two wires, each attached to an electrode, one of which is fastened to the base of the penis and the other designed to fit into the rectum. When a current is turned on, the high frequency impulses stiffen the penis and keep it erect until the power is turned off. As the frequency of the pulses is increased, a forceful ejaculation takes place that can be highly pleasurable—or excruciating.

Because he is highly experimental, he is frequently bisexual. And in heterosexual sex he prefers the exotic and unusual to the conventional. Men born under this sign usually like the French quilled sheath that serves either as a condom or a penis extender. Don't be surprised if he uses a tickler that has a tip in the shape of a devil's head with a protruding red tongue. When he goes exotic, he goes exotic!

His preoccupation with autoeroticism occasionally interferes with his sexual function and contributes to such problems as delayed orgasm and impotency. Too much of his pleasure comes from the conquest, and the actual sex act is secondary.

His taste for novelty and his insatiable curiosity also favor more alarming sexual quirks—such as sadism. When he starts playing with matches, get your clothes on and get out—*fast.*

FIRST MOVES

It's easy to meet them. You may find Aquarius at a party, a study group, or a group-travel tour. Other good meeting places: churches (they can be quite religious), theaters, or concerts (they love music).

They like to surround themselves with people and love organizing get-togethers. If they are guests at someone else's party, you shouldn't have trouble discerning who they are. Look for the magnetic personality, the fascinating conversationalist who, even if surrounded by superficial people, isn't making the usual frivolous small talk. He or she will be discussing ideas and events.

If you don't read much or if you are not able to converse easily, Aquarius may not be for you. How will you keep them interested? Let's suppose you do have something in common. You must be interested in Aquarius or you wouldn't be reading this. How can you get into their good graces?

Well, let's see . . .

You have to make the first suggestion for a date. Keep in mind that Aquarius is basically passive in nature. Don't be timid about asking. Aquarius responds to boldness and confidence. Act as if it were impossible to fail.

For that first date suggest something that's intellectually stimulating—a lecture by a controversial figure; an *avant-garde* film; a stage play by Pinter or Pirandello. You can't go wrong if you start Aquarius's mind ticking. They are very much in tune with the times and keep up on the latest in the arts. Afterward you will find their comments to be both humorous and insightful. Later on, suggest going to an almost forgotten churchyard to read inscriptions on the tombstones. Or perhaps an early-morning visit to the market to watch trucks bringing in the foodstuffs and enjoy that special dish of steamed clams. Always remember that Aquarius does not dig stuffy conventional outings.

They like to give and receive gifts. If you're the giftee, accept with grace. The gifts may probably be a little out of the ordinary but don't seem surprised. As for gifts to give Aquarius: appeal to his mind by giving him a chess or backgammon set, something handcarved and unusual. She likes large striking pieces of jewelry and ultra-sophisticated scents in perfume.

The course of your romance won't run smooth. You can't expect Aquarius to react as ordinary people do. Their antenna are tuned in a different way, that's all, and you can't change it. There will be times when your feelings are hurt by a sudden aloofness, the reasons for which are shrouded in the mystery of personality. Above all, don't probe too deeply into the reasons. That is infringing on their privacy, and Aquarius values privacy highly.

One tip: You've probably been under close study. Some of Aquarius's apparent withdrawal is merely to see you clear from a distance. That's actually encouraging. It means that Aquarius is beginning to think of you as something more than a friend.

EROGENOUS ZONES

The sensitive areas are the calves and ankles. Any position that touches these areas will significantly stimulate desire.

Rub the palm of your hand over the ankle and up the calf with a definite upward motion. Do this caressingly, almost absent-mindedly. You'll be pleased at how Aquarius reacts.

Try making love in a standing position where the woman hooks her calf behind the man's knee and locks her ankle and foot around the man's calf. The natural action during intercourse will cause friction on the erogenous areas. (This is particularly effective in a swimming pool.) Other positions that allow contact with the calf and the ankle will always increase sexual satisfaction.

Aquarius is susceptible to touch when it is gentle. Anything else is a definite turn-off.

LAST MOVES

Want to end it all? Don't fret. Aquarius will probably call it quits first. Their intuitions have warned them long before you heard the message. While you're still listening to the orchestra play, they know the ball is over.

However, if it's a stubborn case, here are some hints that will help you tell an Aquarius that the magic has run out:

Be a homebody. Stay in to watch television rather than go out to meet friends.

Be tight with your purse.

Complain and don't accept advice.

Keep secrets. Aquarius hates to have things hidden.

Scoff at anyone who believes that people act from anything except selfish motives. Deride Aquarius's charitable activities and sympathy for the underprivileged.

When Aquarius makes a mistake, act as if it were unforgivable.

Take the old-fashioned conservative attitude on every possible subject.

Insist on choosing clothes for him or her. Try to cut them off from old friends.

Soon you will have all the privacy you wish. Your Aquarius will have gone. They won't even leave a glass slipper or an old meerschaum pipe to remind you of happier times.

YOUR SENSUAL GUIDE

AQUARIUS and ARIES: There's going to be fun and frolic in the bedroom. Difficulty may arise if either tries to force the other to do anything, for neither can tolerate a domineering partner. They are both imaginative in sex and compatible in other areas. Forceful Aries will take the lead. Chances are excellent either for an affair or more a more lasting relationship.

AQUARIUS and TAURUS: Passionate, highly sexed Taurus finds Aquarius's offhand attitude toward sex baffling. Taurus doesn't want a friend, it wants a mate—while Aquarius is all too prone to make a pal out of its sex partner. Aquarius is also too involved with outside activities to suit home-loving Taurus. Frequent personality clashes between two strong-willed people who can't compromise. Bad vibes for the long term.

AQUARIUS and GEMINI: Aquarius is likely to dominate Gemini, who goes along with its sexual preferences. There will be a great deal of gaiety in the bedroom and little feeling of pressure or passion. Excitable, changeable Gemini finds Aquarius a stabilizing influence. If Gemini becomes interested in Aquarius's outside activities, they will have everything going for them. An interesting affair, a fascinating marriage.

* * *

AQUARIUS and CANCER: Emotional Cancer annoys Aquarius by making sex too important. Aquarius prefers cooler passions and a more casual attitude. In time, Aquarius will feel hemmed in and begin to dislike steadfast, clinging Cancer. Rebuffed, Cancer will grow surly and feel unwanted. An affair has many difficulties. A marriage has very serious problems.

AQUARIUS and LEO: This can become an unholy mess, although for a time it seems to promise exciting adventure. Chief problem: Leo is more physical and Aquarius more interested in the mind. Aquarius is unwilling to offer Leo the kind of sexual worship that natives of that sign demand. Both are independent; Aquarius will resent any attempt by Leo to rule. Sexually responsive, their other problems are too explosive for a long-lasting amour.

AQUARIUS and VIRGO: There is not much sexual attraction between these two. Both have an intellectual outlook—favoring other-than-physical activities. Neither excitement nor initiative is to be found here, for both need more erotic stimulation. Sober, practical Virgo also tends to be critical of expansive, generous Aquarius. A quiet affair will wind down to ennui. A marriage just might survive on common interests outside the bedroom.

AQUARIUS and LIBRA: Both are warm sensitive sexual creatures. Libra's leaning toward erotic games is just what's needed to win Aquarius's wholehearted participation. Each fulfills the other's physical requirements quite satisfactorily. They share other interests also: they both like luxury, enjoy art and music, and freely spend money. The prognosis is for an exciting affair and an unusually happy marriage.

* * *

AQUARIUS and SCORPIO: Scorpio is so jealous and possessive that Aquarius simply can't put up with it. Aquarius is apparently so indifferent to sex that Scorpio's aggressive passions turn toward sadism. Understandably, this increases Aquarius's search for happiness in projects outside the home—away from Scorpio. An affair will be short, a marriage likewise.

AQUARIUS and SAGITTARIUS: Both are unpredictable, lively, and active lovers, which makes for spicy sessions in the bedroom. Their wide-ranging sexual interests feature vivid imagination and the acting out of fantasies. Signs are good in other areas: both are social, like to be away from home, and are interesting, vibrant people who won't be jealous of each other's private lives. Excellent partners for a short- or long-term arrangement.

AQUARIUS and CAPRICORN: Undemonstrative lovers—sexually the combination is likely to be a washout. Capricorn enters physical relationships with caution, and Aquarius isn't likely to be turned on by that approach. Capricorn then considers Aquarius cold and indifferent. Aquarius can't understand provincial, practical, possessive Capricorn. An affair may begin but will go nowhere.

AQUARIUS and AQUARIUS: Admirably suited. Both are inventive lovers and stimulate each other mentally and physically before, during, and after intercourse. They are right on target sexually. However, there is no deep emotional involvement. Both are too rational, sensible, and moderate. They have many interests outside of each other. A pleasant affair, a sound marriage.

AQUARIUS and PISCES: Sexual intimacy between these two soon develops into an emotional tug-of-war with hurt feelings and soap-opera misunderstandings. Sensitive Pisces becomes quite dependent on Aquarius and demands constant proofs of love. Aquarius feels hampered and hindered by the tentacles of its clinging vine. They are at cross-purposes often. An affair may start promisingly but won't go the route.

PISCES

February 19–March 20

THE FEMALE

Ruled by Neptune, planet of beauty and mystery, she is intensely feminine, sensual, intuitive, and responsive. Her powers of insight make her sympathetic to the troubles of others. She never stands on the outside looking in; she actually seems to experience what the other person is feeling, responding to the inner truth more than to outward appearance. Never try to deceive her. She has magical powers to see through to the truth of how things really are.

Because of her unusual sensitivity, she is very drawn to the occult and may make a perceptive palm reader, seer, spiritualist, or medium. Experience has taught her that her "hunches" are psychic in their ability to foretell consequences. Some astrologers believe those born under Pisces are actually spirits returned to the present and that they get precognitive flashes of a future world they departed. That's fanciful, I think, but there's no doubt that both female and male of this sign possess this rare foresight.

Her air of mystery can be deceptive. It's true that she has a strange, haunting quality that invariably attracts men, but she is fundamentally dependent and will attach herself like a barnacle to the person central in her life.

She needs constant reassurance that she is loved. In turn she will repay a mate with the prodigal blessings of a truly sensual nature.

The positive aspects of her sign are not those of action but of dreams and aspirations. She shrinks from the brawling world of conflict and competition. In the struggle for power, her way is subtle. She has an uncanny knack of getting around people—especially influential, important people. Because she appears both innocent and helpless, she draws forth their protective strength. In order to enlist the aid of a man whose support she needs, she will not hesitate to seduce him. She understands and practices the art of using her body to get what she wants.

She falls in love too easily and is dallying with Mr. Wrong when she should be dillying with Mr. Right. Even when happily married, her strong sexual instincts lead her into extra-marital affairs. Her wayward affections are usually sincere, and her expression of love can be delicate, discerning, and charming.

As a rule, she marries gentle and rather undersexed men. She feels safest with them. But in her fervent fantasy life she yearns for another kind of lover, a combination of Lord Byron and a Saracen pirate, a man with a romantic aura, brutal direct ways, and a phallic sword. She longs for this dreamlike suitor to sweep her away from her boylike husband.

Pisces is something of a tease, who will employ all her womanly wiles to capture a new man's interest. This helps her to prove that she is sexually attractive. But she often becomes frightened of the men whose interest she arouses and tries to retreat from their advances. The exceptions are if she ensnares the boy-man type that she has no reason to fear, or if he is the influential type that she needs for some other purpose.

She is an actress who can adapt to any role. She may even play it so well that it becomes hard to distinguish her real personality from the one she takes on, to tell the woman beneath the woman's mask. With that ability and with her active fantasy life, it's obvious that she can make a successful career in theater.

She will be unhappy unless she can somehow combine her sexual fantasies with reality. This often leads her to join sex cults. You will also find Pisces working as a nude model, topless dancer, erotic painter, or writer of sex novels. Some Pisces women become prostitutes. They believe they are serving mankind by offering sexual release to men who can't find it other ways!

However, Pisces woman also makes a good and loving wife, for she possesses the wonderful art of making those around her happy. A good homemaker, she loves children although she tends to spoil them. She is also very capable in handling sick people, and many Pisces women become excellent doctors and nurses.

Unfortunately, something perverse in her nature causes her to pick the wrong kind of man again and again. At times she seems destined to be disappointed in affairs of the heart. This can be dangerous, for her precariously balanced emotional nature cannot stand a prolonged period of stress or unhappiness. That can easily drive her to the brink of nervous collapse.

She is not practical and has little understanding of money matters. She gives gifts in order to buy the acceptance she craves. Inferior people attract her because she senses their need for understanding and help. She will do a favor for anyone who asks—*if* her efforts are appreciated. She sets very high, often unrealistic, standards for those close to her, and will believe in her friends until absolutely compelled by circumstances to alter her faith. Then beware—for she can become vindictive.

HER SEX LIFE

She has a flair for drama in the boudoir. Count on her to make the right moves, say the right things, create the right ambiance. She learns early about sex, and her willingness to please rarely lets her say no.

She is sexually liberated and enjoys a wide range and variety of erotic byplay. It doesn't take much to arouse a Pisces woman. Watching a stag movie or reading the choice parts of a "today" novel will start her breathing heavily. Because she is so suggestible, she will probably try out in the bedroom some of the sexual acrobatics she sees on the screen or reads in the book. It's a good bet that the first sex manual was written by someone born under this sign.

Her natural bent for theatrics helps her to emote with convincing screams and wiggles that whet a lover's appetite. If your fantasies coincide with hers, the action can really get torrid. She will set the scene as though it were a play—proper lighting and musky perfume, black silk underwear, various size vibrators, Chinese dildoes—whatever suits her lover's taste. Once she learns his whims, she uses her imagination to enhance and magnify the situation.

One of the few times that the Pisces woman enjoys the woman-on-top position is on a waterbed, where the motion resembles the calm sea. She is in a swimming position and is able physically and mentally to adjust her muscles for optimum performance.

Her libido is unusually strong at the time of menstruation. With Pisces this may be a psychic or autosuggestive condition. She is strongly susceptible to such influences. At such times she works herself into a sexual passion which is hard for her to control.

An approach used by many Pisces women to find a sexual outlet outside of copulation is the tongue bath. After exciting and stimulating a lover, she will lick his nude body, paying particular attention to erogenous zones—the inside areas of thighs, the navel, or the small of the back upward along the spine. When he is at fever pitch, she starts licking his genitals, particularly the perineum, the space behind the scrotum. When he is fully aroused and ready, she may take him orally and his release will bring her a simultaneous orgasm.

She is easily led into master-slave relationships. She is more apt to welcome rear (anal) entry than any other woman. In fact, she seldom says no to whatever a lover suggests. The bondage rites, the gags, being trussed and fastened to benches, tables, or even hung from the ceiling beams won't turn her off. Sadists and pimps find her amiability a decided asset. Her pliancy encourages those with latent viciousness to work out their sadism at her expense. She will not protest unless she is being hurt beyond endurance. A particular example of this is in the Pisces female's affinity for flagellation.

She has a tendency to a clothes-and-jewelry fetishism. She prefers to wear one or more such items during the sex act: earrings (long pieces that caress her neck as she tosses her head in the love act), rings on her fingers, over-sized bracelets that slide up and down her arms while in the throes of love. Some items of clothing will excite her lover as much as her—such as long nylon stockings, gloves, or French bras and panties that leave her nipples and vagina exposed. If her lover is into the sado-masochistic scene, she will wear a leather vest, a leather mini-skirt or hotpants, and high-heeled boots to excite his interest.

Expect her to cooperate in what others label "abnormal" behavior. Several Pisces women I know say they enjoy "the golden shower" (being urinated on). She will also assume the dominant role if that pleases her lover. One Pisces woman told me this interesting story of her current amour. She would dress up in her fanciest gown, have her hair coiffed, and then meet her lover, who was naked. He then would give her a riding crop and ask her to hit him repeatedly on the buttocks. She did as requested until he got an erection, and continued striking him repeatedly until he ejaculated. His reddened backside inflamed her desires, and she invariably had an orgasm simultaneously with him!

I'll never forget one Pisces woman who came to

me for a consultation. After she had described a particularly perverted sex scene with her current lover, I inquired if she had enjoyed it.

"Absolutely not!" she told me. "I found it disgusting."

"So why did you do it?"

She looked at me in amazement. "He *asked* me to!"

THE MALE

He is passionate, emotional, and unstable. You can expect the unexpected with him. He is constantly pulled by contrary impulses—the symbol of Pisces is two fishes swimming in opposite directions. He is a contradictory personality constantly deciding to do one thing and then doing another.

Unusually sensitive to those around him, he exercises a deep and unconscious magnetic appeal. His nature is warm and responsive, and he sees people not as they are but as he would like them to be. He is most attracted to a sensuous woman, especially if she has a domineering streak. He idealizes the person he loves and will put up with outrageous behavior, for he sees her as one who can do no wrong.

Constantly lured by change and excitement, he yearns for nothing more than emotional stability. He is a dreamer who dreams nothing but impossible dreams. Love must not only be romantic—moonlight and roses and poetry—but also should mean home and contentment and security. Sex is an intimate and private affair, but also world-encompassing, the Grail at the end of the crusader's long search for happiness.

Don't expect too much fidelity. That isn't in his makeup. He is too responsive and too easily influenced. He will convince himself for a time that someone knows what is right for him and has set his course for true north. Then his emotional compass swings wildly to someone else's magnetic appeal.

How can you live with a man who lives so much for the whim of the moment? Be extra sensitive to the swift volatile play of his emotions, and above all be ready to give him the steadying influence of unquestioning love. For him love is the stars and the wide endless heavens; you must make it the roof above his head. If you represent stability to him, you can count on getting him back. He needs that quality in his life.

He is not the marrying kind, however. If a woman does march him off to the altar, someone else is sure to catch his roving eye sooner or later. For him romance is a revolving door that leads both to the minister and the divorce court. He is no respecter of marriage vows—either his own or those of a woman he finds attractive.

He is sensuous, intelligent, unusually creative. A marvelous companion, this man loves to go first class. He is a profligate spender, not thinking about tomorrow, and he indulges himself—and you—never reckoning the cost. He will shower you with expensive presents, perfume, and furs.

Being impressionable, he easily takes on other people's attitudes and habits. If they are nice, he is Mr. Wonderful. If they are drunkards, lock up the liquor cabinet.

When Pisces is well-aspected, he has the advantage of his sensitive sign. He can be idealistic, self-sacrificing, charming. He'll use his superb gifts of creativity as a writer, musician, or artist, but he is not too effective in business. One reason is that he much prefers to work alone; another is that he despises hard work. In most fields of endeavor, if you want to do good work, you have to deliberately take the hard way. Pisces's instinct is to find the easy way. He lacks the practical approach, the organizing ability, and the dynamism of the successful executive. The best place for him is on the creative side, in advertising, public relations, the arts, or anywhere that ideas are more important than the follow-through. He is the kind who prefers to become lost in reflection rather than to find himself in action. He is a procrastinator who simply can't seem to get going.

While articulate, the one thing he cannot do is to call a spade a spade. He will use his mastery of words to avoid making a plain declarative statement. He rarely gives offense, but those who are associated with him rarely know where they stand. He's as hard to come to grips with as a greased pole. You'll eventually discover this is because he has no great convictions. He'll listen to you with what appears to be genuine interest and absorption, but his mind is concentrating on something else entirely or, more probably, just daydreaming. You won't be able to tell the difference. He's too adept at covering up, at giving a performance. He can act as if he's listening better than most people truly listen.

If his sign is afflicted, he can easily sink to the lower depths of drug addiction, alcoholism, depravity. Indeed, he is easily beguiled into any and all vices. He will shift quickly from one perversion to another.

Basically, he lacks confidence in himself and needs to draw support from others like water from a well.

Pisces is the sign of sorrows.

HIS SEX LIFE

He will take the lead in lovemaking and become impatient if he does not get a swift response. He resents having any of his desires questioned—and is offended if you suggest a delay to some more convenient time or place. When he wants you, he's got to have you.

He is inclined to clandestine meetings and secret affairs, often with married women. Indifferent to sexual restrictions both moral and legal, he prefers an experienced partner with a tremendous craving for sexual activity.

He likes to be slowly and admiringly undressed by a woman. He also likes to have sex in a chair, with the woman sitting astride his lap facing him. This posture is ideally adapted to the foreplay at which Pisces male excels, and both will have their hands entirely free for caressing and touching sensitive erotic areas.

I've been told by several Pisces males that they particularly enjoy the fire-and-ice gambit. (It appeals to the contradictory elements in their natures.) A bowl of crushed ice is wrapped in a wet towel and kept handy at bedside. When his passions are ignited to the utmost and the paroxysms of orgasm begin, his partner picks up the wet ice-cold towel and presses it against his crotch, keeping it there until he has spent himself. The shock of cold on the male organ not only stimulates but "freezes" as well and thereby prolongs the orgasm.

Another trick often used by Pisces is to stroke his penis between a woman's feet and roll it over her toes until he can ejaculate in her mouth. Of particular interest to him are a woman's toes. He is definitely one of the "jelly bean boys"—a term applied to admirers of these tiny appendages because of their resemblance to jelly beans. He gets a thrill from seeing a woman's toes, caressing them, sucking on them, particularly through a nylon casing. (Don't knock this until you've tried it!)

Pisces male strives to make his erotic fantasies and dreams come true. Most of these fantasies revolve around a dominant woman who makes excessive and unreasonable and often faintly repellent demands on him and his vain attempts to satisfy her.

A favorite technique: While the woman lies over him, he will lick and suck on one breast and leave a heavy residue of saliva. Then he moves his mouth to the other nipple as he uses his fingers to rub and tweak the first nipple. The saliva gives her the feeling that two mouths are working on her breasts, doubling her pleasure. And in pleasing her, he gets his own satisfaction.

Sadists and masochists will find him willing to play any role they desire. He aims to please. If his lover wants him to dress as a woman, he will put on her bra and panties, stockings, shoes, and gloves. If she wants him as a baby, he will put on diapers and rubber panties. If she wants to humiliate him, spank him, or discipline him, she will meet with no serious objection. He will kneel, kiss her feet, do exactly what she tells him.

If his woman likes to be watched performing the sex act, he will oblige by standing behind a screen to give her and her lover an encouraging word at a crucial juncture. Or he will be the third party to a triad (a transient affair) or to a troilism (a permanent arrangement), where he performs cunnilingus, anilingus, fellatio, and pederasty.

He is the one who will accept a soaped enema and hold the water within by an effort of will while he goes through foreplay, intercourse, and afterplay. The mounting pressure on his bowels adds to the final orgasmic release. One Pisces male had a rather sadistic mate who insisted on bringing him to orgasm again orally before allowing him to go to the bathroom.

Another way in which Pisces gets the same effect is by drinking large amounts of water or beer before a sexual bout. Refraining from urinating increases the pressure on the bladder and, in turn, increases the pleasure at orgasm. Pisces will cheerfully accept pain with pleasure if the pleasure is great enough or if it excites his partner.

His erotic fantasies also lead him toward exotic masturbation, sometimes featuring quite elaborate life-size rubber dolls that can be turned and twisted at will, or close-fitting suction cups that can be used in the privacy of his car while driving.

A favorite trick of Pisces man is to place a tight rubber band at the base of his penis after he attains an erection. This not only preserves the erection for a longer period but gives him a delightful pain-pleasure sensation at the point of ejaculation.

Pisces male is the sexual patsy of the zodiac. He will become addicted to anything that will give him pleasure and release. His hang-ups are anything that stimulate his pain-pleasure reflex. Most of them enjoy having their ears nibbled or their flesh lightly raked with fingernails, or even getting love bites on the genitals. But in extreme cases Pisces males must draw blood to achieve orgasm or indulge in anal intercourse or even, in one case I know of, make small nicks with razor blades and then suck the wounds.

FIRST MOVES

You'll find Pisces in the center of a social occasion, usually surrounded by admirers. Their customary charm of manner and indolent good nature attracts people to them. In fact, if Pisces isn't being admired, he or she will probably be sulking in a corner.

A good opening remark would be a comment on theater, motion pictures, television, or any entertainment art. That captures Pisces's interest at once, for they all (whatever their present occupation) want to be actors, writers, or artists. Another sure way to capture their attention is to start discussing the occult—particularly anything involving reincarnation. Many Pisceans believe their souls have gone through previous lifetime cycles. Those who don't actually believe that will be fascinated to talk about it.

Once you've got them started, by all means let Pisces monopolize the conversation. If you're ignorant on the subject, Pisces will be only too willing to help you understand. There's nothing they like better.

First date? Suggest a restaurant that offers dancing. Pisces loves dancing, both social and solo. Or perhaps follow up on their interest in the occult by suggesting a tea-leaf reading, a seance, or an evening at home trying to make a Ouija board talk. On each occasion be sure to greet them with a compliment. They badly need reassurance.

Don't offer a cocktail before the meal unless you know that your particular Pisces can handle it. Too often they can't. People born under the fish sign do have a hankering for liquids—anything from ice-cold water to hot tea—but alcohol spells trouble for them. There is a higher percentage of alcoholics under this sign than any other.

They also have rather poor dietary habits, so you will be doing them a favor if you take control in that area. Their health tends to be a bit fragile, and you can help them get rid of these bad habits. Adopt a positive, enthusiastic attitude for health regimens, encourage them in preventive medicines, and you will not only make Pisces healthier and happier but fulfill their not-so-secret need for a strong protector and adviser.

If you're giving gifts, Pisces woman responds to the colors of the sea: pale green, aquamarine, and misty blue. Scarves or clothing in those colors appeal to her. For him try a good in-depth biography, a book on the occult, poetry, or Shakespeare.

When matters reach a point where you need an ideal setting for lovemaking, here's a valuable tip: A warm place with the movement of water always delights Pisces. So try an electric blanket on your water-bed. Or find a nice private whirlpool bath big enough for two.

EROGENOUS ZONES

The feet. Pisces will respond to gentle massage and caressing of the heel and arch, delicate stroking with a feather on the sole, or sucking on each toe. Beginning at the ankle bone, use a circular motion with your fingertips around to the top of the foot and then down to the toes. If you rub the toes between the pads of your fingers or take them in your mouth and softly bite them, you will drive a Pisces mad with delight.

Pisces woman likes to masturbate a male lover with her feet. She does this by gently rolling his penis between the balls of her feet. The male Pisces gets added stimulation by inserting his toe into the woman's vagina or just rubbing his feet over the vaginal and anal area.

Soaking the feet before any sexual exercise makes Pisces more receptive.

LAST MOVES

When the time comes to "end it all," you may have a bit of trouble. Pisces is ultra-sensitive, easily hurt. But if you screw up your courage to the sticking point, you can push matters to a conclusion. Here are some ways that you can grease the chute:

Neglect Pisces when in company, interrupting their conversations, or holding them up to ridicule.

Become argumentative, sloppy in your dress, and monopolize the conversation without giving them a chance to express their ideas.

Skip praise and suggest that they need improvement. For example, why don't they change the color of their hair?

Return all their gifts to the store. Become a tightpurse with money.

Scold Pisces over trivial things. Be impatient with mistakes. Upset their old-fashioned values.

You'll soon have a sullen, morose Pisces on your hands. And in this mood, there's nothing for them to do but look for comfort elsewhere.

Your clinging vine will find someone else to cling to.

YOUR SENSUAL GUIDE

PISCES and ARIES: Dynamic Aries unlocks Pisces's full potential in the bedroom. Aries, of course, dominates —but this is what Pisces is looking for. However, tact is necessary for the combination to work in other areas. Pisces is very sensitive to criticism, and Aries is frequently blunt. If they work out their differences, this can be a sexy, enduring relationship.

PISCES and TAURUS: They are almost equally passionate, but highly sensitive Pisces needs the kind of special consideration not often forthcoming from down-to-earth Taurus. Far more emotional and sentimental, Pisces is likely to suffer from hurt feelings if taken too matter-of-factly. If this problem can be overcome, there's a good chance this combination will work. A sensual affair, a satisfactory marriage.

PISCES and GEMINI: Two unstable signs make an unpromising sexual combination. There may be physical attraction, but Gemini is too changeable and Pisces too sensitive for it to last. Gemini's thoughtlessness will offend Pisces. Both are so egocentric that there will be little attempt made at an accommodation. They need stronger, more dominant partners. A short, possibly heated affair; a quite infelicitous marriage.

PISCES and CANCER: Cancer is likely to prove a demanding lover, but Pisces won't object to that. Sexually both are demonstrative and may spend a good deal of time in the bedroom. Cancer takes the lead and makes most decisions. Despite some quarrels, on the whole they satisfy each other's emotional needs and are careful of the other's sensitivity. A highly compatible couple.

PISCES and LEO: Fire and water do not mix. Outgoing Leo is frustrated by introspective Pisces, even in the bedroom. Neither quite understands the other. Sentimental Pisces begins to pall on Leo and drives it to seek satisfaction elsewhere. Pisces languishes at home dreaming its sad dreams while Leo roams abroad. An affair will be difficult, marriage will be unrewarding.

PISCES and VIRGO: Overly affectionate Pisces does not get much satisfaction from reserved Virgo. Virgo resists Pisces's excessive sexual demands and turns hypercritical and faultfinding. There are other problems too. Practical, logical Virgo won't indulge Pisces's extravagant tastes or put up with its emotional waywardness. Virgo will make plans while Pisces acts on the spur of the moment—then changes its mind. A quarrelsome affair, a joyless marriage.

PISCES and LIBRA: They have difficulty in relating to each other except in a physical way. If they hit it off there, chances are still dim that it will develop into anything worthwhile. Libra won't supply the kind of dominance that Pisces needs. Both like luxury, but neither is willing to work hard to achieve it. A disjointed affair, a marriage that eventually turns bitter.

* * *

PISCES and SCORPIO: They should enjoy a deep and satisfying physical union. Excellently matched as lovers, Scorpio's strength provides the firm support that Pisces needs in other areas. Pisces will not provoke Scorpio's jealousy and construes Scorpio's possessiveness as a form of love—which it is. Both quickly ignite as lovers and find complete gratification. The sooner these two take the vows the happier they'll be.

PISCES and SAGITTARIUS: They may have their moments erotically speaking, but Sagittarius is independent and venturesome, and Pisces, sensing this, becomes ever more dependent and emotionally clutching. Pisces's languorous lovemaking is simply a bore to restless Sagittarius, who wants to move on to other interests. Sagittarius will be tempted to provoke and mock Pisces's sentimental yearnings. An affair will end almost as soon as it begins, a marriage would be disastrous.

PISCES and CAPRICORN: A fine sexual pairing. There may be minor problems and misunderstandings, but these two are well equipped to work through to a solution. Strong, dominant Capricorn knows how to make Pisces feel desirable and secure. Pisces, in turn, brings a breath of romance into stolid Capricorn's emotional life. Their differences complement each other and assure a very good affair or marriage.

PISCES and AQUARIUS: Sexually they may find each other stimulating for a time, for both are imaginative lovers. But self-centered, subjective Pisces has little in common with outward-directed, social Aquarius. Independent and determined Aquarius won't waste precious effort to bolster and reassure Pisces. Aquarius tries to solve problems with logic, Pisces with emotion. And the problems will defeat them in the long run.

PISCES and PISCES: Mutual empathy provides a wonderful understanding of each other's sexual needs. If their problems could be absorbed by sheer physical compatibility, this would be one of the zodiac's best matches. However, these emotional leeches soon drain each other's reserves. Without a strong, dominant partner they go off in wrong directions. A highly sensual affair, but marriage will end in increasing sexual indulgence and possible depravity.